Praise for
The Short List

"*The Short List* demonstrates how a small collection of deep, meaningful relationships can transform your career. David Ackert makes a compelling case for quality over quantity in this incredibly useful relationship manual. Reading this book is one of the highest ROI investments you can make in yourself."

—WILLIAM O'NEIL, Chicago Managing Partner, Winston & Strawn LLP

"'When looking for new clients, fill a suite, not the whole stadium.' David Ackert's practical approach to narrowing your scope to those few people that will make or break your year is critical to long-term success in generating revenue and building an impactful, engaging practice. Less effort, more results."

—DARRYL CROSS, US Executive Sales Coach, Norton Rose Fulbright

"With so many options and opinions about how to ignite a successful practice, it can be hard to know which tactics to employ. With *The Short List*, David takes the guess work out of where to start. He offers practical guidance about how to anchor your business development efforts in strengthening the relationships that bring both joy and opportunity."

—JULIA BENNETT, Chief Marketing and
Business Development Officer, Davis Wright Tremaine LLP

"For the busy professional, the task of managing a vast and ever-evolving network can feel overwhelming. In *The Short List*, David Ackert provides a step-by-step guide to turn your network into a strategic, manageable pipeline system that helps you identify the key people you need to prioritize and the techniques you can use to turn those relationships into business referrals. This book is an indispensable resource."

—MICHAEL RIVERA, Chief Strategy Officer,
Association for Corporate Growth (ACG)

"This book is spot on, showing people how to effectively use their time to develop the right relationships to build their businesses. As a business development partner at Withum and President of Provisors (a nationwide networking organization), I build relationships for a living. And yet I still gather tips and ideas from David Ackert."

— **STEVEN M. MARTINI,** MST, CPA, Partner, Withum

"'Elevating sales for service professionals.' *The Short List* is perfect for those who value a strategic approach to sales. It transforms the dated high-volume prospecting methods into a refined system focused on high-value opportunities. With David Ackert's relatable tone, compelling research, and clear step-by-step guidance, this book is a must-have for anyone who resonates with the idea of a high-quality, buyer-first approach."

— **SAMANTHA MCKENNA,** CEO, SamSales Consulting

"David Ackert has distilled decades of business development experience into a concise, practical guide that shows you exactly where to direct your efforts. If you want to elevate your networking strategy and see real results, *The Short List* is your roadmap to success."

— **NIR EYAL,** *Wall Street Journal* best-selling author of *Hooked: How to Build Habit-Forming Products*

"As a managing partner, I know that deep client relationships are the foundation of every firm's success. *The Short List* expertly highlights the importance of focusing on key individuals within our networks and explains how to activate these connections. The result is a blueprint for targeted and personalized business development. An essential guide for every professional."

— **PATRICK A. ROGERS,** Managing Partner, Hinckley Allen

"Every rainmaker knows that their success is built on the strategic cultivation of a small network of deep, high-impact relationships. With *The Short List*, David Ackert has delivered the essential guidebook for business development results by laying out a clear, actionable roadmap for growing and maintaining your own high performing network. *The Short List* should be on every ambitious business leader's desk."

—**BRIAN NAPACK,** Executive Chairman, 2U; former CEO, John Wiley & Sons; former Chairman, Association of American Publishers; former President, Macmillan

"An easy and compelling read, *The Short List* is packed with focused exercises and templates that provide practical, actionable value. It is a rare gem—a succinct yet sophisticated business guide that offers insights and practical strategies valuable to a range of professionals from those in the nascent stages of their careers to those in C-level roles."

—**TRICIA LILLEY,** Chief Marketing and Business Development Officer, Barnes & Thornburg LLP

"Among the many reasons I loved *The Short List* is that David Ackert doesn't gloss over the fears and uneasiness that hold so many professionals back from growing their practice and, in the process, expanding the reach of their impact. David shares the plans, actions, and exercises he uses to hone his message and execute his strategies, making him one of our industry's most respected, admired, and short-listed people."

—**PATRICK FULLER,** Chief Strategist, Legal, ALM

"David distills his extensive and unique experience into a practical playbook with tools anyone can use to initiate the growth of their business or enhance existing success. "The Short List" is an essential resource for anyone looking to achieve significant business development results. I am excited to add The Short List to my key reference materials."

—**CHRISTOPHER R. HEDICAN,** Managing Partner, Baird Holm, LLP

"A clear, achievable roadmap to focused growth and faster success. *The Short List* removes complexity from client development, unlocks opportunity, and ultimately is a guide to greater personal fulfillment."

—**JUSTIN PORTAZ,** Chief Marketing Officer, Jenner & Block LLP

"*The Short List* offers practical, research-based methods to deliver greater returns on business development activities. Often professionals spread themselves too thin, don't know when and how to get a contact to a sale, or feel unsure of where to start. Ackert provides strategies for all three. If you're serious about growing your book of business, you'll want to put *The Short List* on your short list of books to read."

—**KELLY HARBOUR,** Chief Business Development Officer, Goulston & Storrs

"Everyone seems to agree that successful business development plans begin and end with relationships. That revelation, however, is not enough to answer the questions "What should I do first?" and "What should I do next?" David Ackert answers those questions. *The Short List* is a thorough and practical guide to demystifying the inevitably rewarding world of smart business development strategies."

—**PATRICK F. COURTEMANCHE,** Chief Marketing and Business Development Officer, Dorsey & Whitney LLP

"David Ackert has already proven that he is one of our industry's great consultants, a savvy executive coach, and highly regarded business development thought leader. Now he has crafted an amazing book that resonates and enlightens readers on how to build effective and rewarding business networks and relationships in a practical and tactical way."

—**JUSTIN EDMONDSON,** Director of Client Development, Duane Morris LLP

"David Ackert has been known in our industry for practical and insightful discussions around effective business development. Taking his famous 'fishbowl' conversations now to print, David's book provides the roadmap for becoming a successful rainmaker."

—**CHRISTIE CÁCERES,** Chief Business Development
and Marketing Officer, Sheppard Mullin

"Converting casual relationships into quality referral sources is the key to keeping the business development pipeline flush with opportunity. Yet, many professional service firms do not know how. In this book, David teaches the reader that process."

—**GREG ALEXANDER,** Founder, Collective 54

"I was an early adopter of David Ackert's systematic approach to business development, and it was instrumental to the successful consulting firm I run today. Read *The Short List* if you don't want to spend a lot of unnecessary time and energy doing it the hard way."

—**JAMEY HARVEY,** CEO, Agilian

THE
SHORT
LIST

David Ackert

THE SHORT LIST

How to Drive

Business Development by

Focusing on the People

Who Matter Most

GREENLEAF
BOOK GROUP PRESS

Published by Greenleaf Book Group Press
Austin, Texas
www.gbgpress.com

Distributed by Greenleaf Book Group

For ordering information or special discounts for bulk purchases, please contact Greenleaf Book Group at PO Box 91869, Austin, TX 78709, 512.891.6100.

Illustrations in chapter 13 by William Lebeda
Design and composition by Greenleaf Book Group and Mimi Bark
Cover design by Greenleaf Book Group and Anna Jordan

Publisher's Cataloging-in-Publication data is available.

Print ISBN: 979-8-88645-298-3

eBook ISBN: 979-8-88645-299-0

To offset the number of trees consumed in the printing of our books, Greenleaf donates a portion of the proceeds from each printing to the Arbor Day Foundation. Greenleaf Book Group has replaced over 50,000 trees since 2007.

Printed in the United States of America on acid-free paper

25 26 27 28 29 30 31 32   10 9 8 7 6 5 4 3 2 1

First Edition

The Short List is dedicated to those who take the time to mentor others, including those who mentored me over the years, and Arrod, for allowing me to mentor him.

Contents

Foreword

As the faculty chair of multiple executive programs at Harvard's business and law schools, I'm often struck by how seemingly straightforward ideas can have a transformative effect on seasoned practitioners when they are presented in a compelling framework and have a raft of practical "how-to" points alongside. Such is the concept of *The Short List: How to Drive Business Development by Focusing on the People Who Matter Most*.

This idea is also at the heart of my research and advisory work based on smarter collaboration. When we concentrate on building higher-quality networks, not necessarily bigger ones, we have a ripe ground for higher-value, more goal-aligned projects. These "collaborators" are not haphazardly chosen; their inclusion on our Short List is deliberate and tactical. David points out that "most of us have too few of the right people in our networks." My fifteen-plus years of research at Harvard and with hundreds of clients across professional services firms backs this up. We often foster ties with people just like us (a risk known as "homophily" in the world of psychology) or whose backgrounds do not align with where we want to be professionally (maybe an old friend who's never moved away from home). If time were an infinite resource, okay. But it's not and we must be intentional.

Enter *The Short List.* According to David, people who focus on the nine to thirty-five highest-opportunity relationships—whether clients, connectors, or prospects—consistently see their books of business increase significantly within about twelve months (including many who double the value of their client base). This range is supported by Dunbar's Number and the Pareto Principle, which together suggest that only 20 percent of your 150 closest connections have the potential to help you succeed. Of these, 10 to 20 percent should be perfect strangers.

These numbers definitely resonate. In my advisory work I frequently see the benefits of clients focusing business development efforts on a relatively small number of accounts. These accounts have the biggest potential for sophisticated, multi-service line engagements and collaboration. That said, they should not be chosen willy-nilly. Just like Short List contacts, they should be selected based on key objectives, their value vis-à-vis those objectives, and other factors that evolve over time (which means we need to regularly revisit our prioritization).

David emphasizes that our Short Lists must advance our SMART goals and possess four characteristics: positive chemistry, meaningful character, the right level of competence, and a spirit of collaboration. These make total sense. My organizational research unequivocally shows that interpersonal trust, competence trust, and collaboration skills are top ingredients for effective collaboration and its data-backed benefits—including higher revenue and profit, faster innovation, and deeper client relationships.

But David reminds us that these requirements may take on different flavors, depending on one's relationship category. While connectors need to exhibit strong competence, clients' and prospects' lack of knowledge in certain areas is exactly why you are seeking to serve them. In these cases, *you* need to show your expertise and bandwidth.

While reading *The Short List*, I was struck by the number of simple yet effective exercises for readers. These exercises help you create an initial Short List, refine it over time, and cultivate new Short List candidates. This cultivation step involves 1) developing a brand to attract candidates, and 2) more actively seeking out new candidates.

I appreciate David's acknowledgement that both branding and relationship-building play a vital role in business development. All too often, I have found that professionals dismiss the value of LinkedIn, content creation, and other thought leadership efforts. They forget (or ignore) that a carefully crafted brand—one that communicates with your target audience—is an essential avenue to reach the people and opportunities that fulfill your goals.

David and I agree that a personal elevator pitch is a particularly useful branding exercise: not only can it be used in a networking context, but also as the basis for a LinkedIn post, website bio, or presentation. He specifies that this pitch should cover what you do, who you help, how you help, and what you do in your free time. I don't always bring in my personal interests but appreciate the tip that it can help people relate to you, paving the way for follow-up conversations.

For more active, individual-focused relationship development, David makes the case for giving genuine, *specific* compliments (centered on accomplishments, inherent traits, and competencies). These activate the same part of the brain as a monetary reward and "fulfill our basic human need for social acceptance." I agree about the value of kind words but will add that you shouldn't shy away from healthy conflict once a relationship has been established. People across influence levels will appreciate your honest input on potential issues or concerns. Differing opinions, and managing them effectively, are at the heart of smarter collaboration and its financial (and other) outcomes.

When it comes to adding complete strangers to your Short List, David has a specific exercise that prompts you to note the characteristics (demographics, psychographics, and service needs) of your current versus prospective high-value clients. This makes sense to me. If you are just relying on expertise from people you know, you are missing out on fresh and differentiated insights that can help you take your performance to the next level.

Another key message: make sure you're playing a long game. Someone might not respond for a while. Don't take it personally, but instead realize that when the timing is right, they will most likely help you out. I tell this to my clients, too. While the best relationships involve give and take, you must take a bigger-picture view and not let a single request or moment determine the relationship's quality. David helps us adopt this approach by providing a buying-stages framework, full of norms and tips for each stage.

Much of the guidance revolves around proactive moves that people can make. This delights me because proactivity is what differentiates the best professional services providers from the crowd. By seeing around corners, collaborating with a wide range of people to gain insights, and enthusiastically sharing these insights with clients (even outside of formal engagements), you are showing your knowledge *and* dedication. David rounds out this discussion with practical advice for leveraging connectors, including steps for establishing advisory roundtables that deepen these relationships, promote the exchange of valuable information, and boost referral activity.

The common thread throughout *The Short List* is that your business development network and activities should be purposeful; David offers many to-dos and worksheets to help you make this happen. This reflective, pragmatic approach highly aligns with smarter collaboration; as such, I believe that business development professionals across professional services markets would benefit from the science, stories, and wisdom within this book. Consider using it as a tool during a workshop, retreat, or budget planning session—it's a good starting point for a wider growth strategy. As for me, I will find ways to apply some of the ideas in my smarter collaboration work.

—DR. HEIDI K. GARDNER

Quality Over Quantity

You can have whatever you want in business if you know the right people. Want to fly first class for free? You'll need to know someone who works at the airline. Want a high-paying job at that airline? You'll need a connection at the corporate office. Want funding for your startup? You'll need a network of investors. Want to land that Fortune 500 client? You'll need a relationship with the decision-makers at the company, or a referral source who is willing to make the introduction.

Whether it's launching a new endeavor, acquiring a new client, getting a new job, fulfilling a charitable mission, or enhancing your visibility in a given industry, it all comes down to having the right conversations at the right time with the right people. So, when you start adding those people to your network, establishing a mutually beneficial relationship with them, and engaging in authentic, persuasive conversations, the results you want come to fruition.

Unfortunately, most of us have too few of the right people in our networks. We have 500+ first-degree connections on LinkedIn, most of whom we've never met. We receive hundreds of emails every day, mostly from people we don't know, trying to sell us things we don't want. We have a thousand "friends" on Facebook and Instagram, a hundred acquaintances we rarely see, and an inner circle of a few dozen people who are mostly unable to help us achieve our professional goals.

What's wrong with this picture?

DISCONNECTED IN THE DIGITAL AGE

A study published by the Harvard Graduate School of Education found that young people are significantly lonelier than those of older generations, despite the fact that Millennials, Gen Z, and Gen Alpha are the most frequent users of social media.[1] It's ironic that an increasingly interconnected world only dilutes our interpersonal connections. After all, it's nearly impossible to maintain meaningful relationships when they number in the hundreds or thousands. There simply isn't enough time in the day.

This disconnectedness has decreased our willingness to communicate. Over the last decade spammers have made billions of robocalls, and all too often, scammed people under false pretenses. The effect on the broader culture is that most people have learned to mistrust phone calls. According to Pew Research Center, more than 80 percent of all calls in the US now go unanswered.[2] Similarly, over 122

---

1   "Loneliness in America: How the Pandemic Has Deepened an Epidemic of Loneliness and What We Can Do About It," *Harvard Graduate School of Education*, February 2021, https://mcc.gse.harvard.edu/reports/loneliness-in-america.

2   Colleen McClain, "Most Americans Don't Answer Cellphone Calls from Unknown Numbers," *Pew Research Center*, December 14, 2020, https://www.pewresearch.org/short-reads/2020/12/14/most-americans-dont-answer-cellphone-calls-from-unknown-numbers/.

billion spam emails are sent out every day, but for every 12.5 million spam emails sent, only one person responds.[3] There is a cyberattack every thirty-nine seconds.[4] Deepfakes and other AI-generated experiences are becoming more and more undetectable. Technology has scaled many things in our lives, including distrust.

So how can we authentically connect with people in an increasingly crowded, noisy, dangerous, and untrustworthy world? The answer, and the topic of this book, is this: focus on quality over quantity.

THE SHORT LIST: A MORE INTENTIONAL NETWORK

The Short List is a system for creating a more intentional network of trusted relationships, prioritized according to their ability to help you achieve your goals. This book will show you how to focus your network down to the most crucial people, and ensure you provide each other with meaningful value. When you put some care into selecting the people you interact with and ensure the number isn't unmanageable, you make business development easier, with more sustainable outcomes.

You don't have to be a serial networker or a social extrovert to manage a Short List. But you do have to be thoughtful and selective about the people with whom you choose to spend your time.

I discovered the Short List through trial and error. Before I was the CEO of a successful business development enablement company, I was a television actor, working on shows like *The West Wing*, *Monk*, *CSI: Miami*, and *Bones*. Like many industries, Hollywood is

---

3   Nikolina Cveticanin, "Wht's [sic] on the Other Side of Your Inbox—20 SPAM Statistics for 2024," *DataProt*, February 6, 2024, https://dataprot.net/statistics/spam-statistics/.

4   Jacob Fox, "Top Cybersecurity Statistics for 2024," *Cobalt*, December 8, 2023, https://www.cobalt.io /blog/cybersecurity-statistics-2024.

a "who you know" town, so when I first arrived in Los Angeles, I set
out to expand my network with as many people as possible. I talked
to strangers, attended events, asked for introductions, volunteered for
charities, and tried to befriend anyone who was willing to talk to
me. But most of the people I met were ultimately only interested
in forwarding their own agendas. Very few of them placed value on
friendship, unless it was a friend who could help with their career
ambitions. And in those instances, when I *was* able to help them
succeed, many of them were unwilling to return the favor.

My interactions with these people were frustrating, and sometimes even painful. One such experience involved a fellow actor. We
had a great rapport, and an exciting idea for a film, so we decided to
pool our resources and collaborate. We spent a lot of time writing
the script, building momentum, and getting the right people committed to the project. Because I trusted him, and believed in what
we were doing together, I called in all my personal favors and even
invested money I didn't have into the project. But once it became clear
that our project was not going to take off, my friend became distant.
Suddenly he was too busy to return a call or to grab a beer. It wasn't
long before he stopped communicating with me altogether. Of course,
I understood that he needed to prioritize his next opportunity, but
I was deeply disappointed to learn that he had no interest in sustaining even a casual connection with me unless there was a direct
benefit to his career. I was devastated by the loss of someone I once
considered a dear friend.

This experience taught me to be more discerning with my network; to surround myself with people possessing a deeper sense of
character, who genuinely wanted to be helpful, even when there
was no immediate reward. People willing to play the long game and
invest in a network of like-minded allies, recognizing that, as long as

the right characteristics were in place, we would eventually find ways to help each other succeed.

I realized that it would be much more rewarding to build professional relationships with those who were willing to explore how we might be able to help each other, and as we discovered ways to do so, follow through. They, and only they, would earn a place on my Short List.

THE SHORT LIST IS ESSENTIAL WHEN YOU'RE SHORT ON TIME.

I retired from acting but retained the lessons I learned about how people behave and how they communicate their needs. I began an inquiry into the art and science of relationship development and how it applies in business, earned a master's in psychology to better understand human behavior, and became certified as a business coach. As I started working with clients in a range of industries, I discovered that the Short List concept resonated most in the professional services space, where expert advisors rely on their networks to build successful legal, accounting, consulting, and engineering practices. These busy timekeepers sought me out to coach them through an efficient way to harness their limited business development time into meaningful results. When they identified and prioritized their Short Lists, their books of business outpaced those of their competitors.

Regardless of your line of work, or the things you want to accomplish in your life, you'll find that a Short List will accelerate your progress. If you reflect on past achievements, you'll see that there were a few people who were instrumental in your success. (Perhaps you think of them as your inner circle.) Chances are you encountered them out of happenstance—working at the same firm, participating in the same group, enrolled in the same school, or participating on a board—rather than through a conscious decision to surround yourself with a select group who are perfectly positioned to care about your success and advance your professional goals.

It's only human to take the path of least resistance. But in professional networking, when the two paths that lie before us are, "sift through my three thousand Outlook contacts to try to find new opportunities" or "put it off until later," it's obvious which one most of us prefer to do. This book will place another convenient, and far more effective, option in place: "Reconnect with a handful of the most influential people I know and like."

The Short List is for anyone who recognizes that the best way to achieve success is through meaningful, purposeful interactions with people they trust. By the end of this book, you will understand three things:

1. How to gain more business opportunities through the people you already have in your network.

2. Who you need to add to your network so you can achieve your goals.

3. How to apply a systematic approach to business development that takes less time and yields better results.

If you are a busy professional, this book will help you accelerate your business development results. I've included exercises and worksheets to help you put your Short List into action. If you're already a successful rainmaker, you can use *The Short List* to refine and systematize your approach. If you're a firm leader, this book will help you understand how to enhance your firm's business development culture and drive more topline growth. A student of business development will find new techniques in this book to add to their arsenal. And if you are stuck at a plateau, you can use *The Short List* to advance your book of business to the next stage.

The principles in this book are consistent with the actions successful rainmakers take. Rainmakers eliminate nonessential distractions and prioritize essential relationships. They play to their strengths. They regularly dedicate energy toward business development. Follow the principles in *The Short List*, and like other successful businesspeople, you will generate exceptional results. You will save a dozen years of wasted time, hundreds of unproductive meetings, and thousands of superficial conversations that lead nowhere. *The Short List* is the key to millions in additional revenue and a network full of relationships that actually matter to you.

So, let's get started.

PART 1

Creating and Optimizing a Short List

Chapter 1

A Winning Strategy

In most romantic comedies, there is the inevitable blind date montage, where our protagonist sits across from various oddballs and tries to force their way through awkward interactions. The oblivious blind date can't stop bragging about how great they are. The creepy one asks inappropriate questions. And the pushy one wants to go too far too fast.

For me, that's what professional networking felt like. When I transitioned out of the entertainment industry and started my career as a business coach, I knew I needed to build a new platform, so I joined several networking groups and attended any event that would have me. I lunched with countless accountants, bankers, consultants, entrepreneurs, executives, financial advisors, lawyers, and hopefuls, trying to find commonalities that held our mutual interest. We struggled through niceties, fished for synergies, and eventually just wished the server would hurry up and bring us the check.

The process was tedious and inefficient. So, I decided I would only propose meetings with people whose company I genuinely enjoyed. These meetings were more fun, and our intention to help each other was more genuine. But over time I discovered that, unless we were both committed to a mutually beneficial dynamic, the upside was strictly social. Connecting with people I liked and wanted to help made professional networking feel less like a string of bad blind dates, but I was still missing a key ingredient for success: influence.

The more I networked with people I liked, the more my connections consisted of individuals whose interests, demographics, and aspirations were similar to my own. This made it easy for us to relate to one another, but it also meant that we shared the same limitations and lack of resources and were unable to be of much help to one another.

I came from a modest working-class background. My circle of influence was like a flat line that stretched horizontally across my cohort, which was why it was so difficult to advance vertically. That's when I started to realize that the people in my life represented the scope of opportunities that were immediately available to me.

Over time, I observed that whenever a meaningful business opportunity or job offer came my way, it originated from a client, mentor, or connector from the upper echelon in my network. Simply put, they had more influence within their organizations and communities than I did. I also realized that these influential contacts were much more inclined to help me if they saw that I could somehow contribute to *their* success, and the more that I tried to help them, the more they looked out for me. So, focusing more of my time on influential people whose goals were aligned with my own was clearly a winning strategy.

HOW MANY RELATIONSHIPS SHOULD I CULTIVATE?

Even with my more strategic intention in mind, I still struggled with scope. How many influential people did I need in my network, and how many could I realistically maintain? Dunbar's Number helped me answer this question.

English evolutionary psychologist Robin Dunbar summarized his research in his book *Friends*, illustrating an upper threshold when it comes to the number of relationships most people can actively manage. Across the board, he found that the average size of a cohesive network of friends is 150 people. Think of it as the number of people in our lives we would feel comfortable approaching (and whose names we might remember) if we randomly ran into them on the street. Most of us do not have the time or energy to maintain any more than 150 relationships.

Dunbar arrived at this conclusion initially by researching the behavior patterns of primates, tribal societies, and early medieval villages. He discovered that the average size of a cohesive community is approximately 150 people. He then looked to contemporary social patterns and discovered that the same phenomenon plays out in the modern era. When you receive a holiday card, count yourself among the lucky 150—that's the average number of cards people mail to their contacts every year. The average Facebook user interacts with around 150 "friends." Dunbar references a study conducted at the University of Copenhagen, where researchers examined over 23 million emails sent by approximately 5,600 professionals over a three-month period. Based on whether emails were replied to, they were able to conclude the number of reciprocal relationships people maintain. It too was consistent with Dunbar's Number.

Most single-office professional services firms branch off into new geographies when their timekeeper headcount exceeds 150. Any larger and they struggle to sustain the cultural cohesion that protects against competitor poaching, or subgroups splintering off to start smaller boutiques.

Now, to arrive at your Short List, consider the 80/20 rule, or the Pareto Principle, named after economist Vilfredo Pareto. The 80/20 rule suggests that for most endeavors, 80 percent of the results are a product of 20 percent of the causes. In other words, only 20 percent of your 150 closest connections have the potential to help you succeed. **That brings the list down to just thirty people.**

This is the organizing principle I used to focus my business development energy. There were times when my Short List was more concentrated, but it mostly hovered somewhere between ten and thirty.

DOES A SHORT LIST WORK? IT DID FOR ME.

Applied over time, my Short List enabled me to go from former Hollywood actor to struggling solo practitioner to CEO of a multi-million-dollar enterprise. We attracted highly skilled, executive-level business development coaches to our team, we developed a proprietary SaaS product that we license to firms all over the world, we launched a contract staffing division, we started working with global brands like Disney, Warner Bros. Discovery, URW (the international company behind the Westfield shopping malls), multi-national financial institutions, Big Four accounting firms, and some of the largest law firms in the world. We coached our clients on how to create and leverage a Short List, helping them grow their books of business to new heights.

Each of these successes came down to a conversation with some-one who was on my Short List at the time. Certainly, there were steps leading up to that moment, but ultimately, the game-changing result was a function of a single interaction with an influential person at each of these organizations. And once I established these relation-ships, I developed a system to maintain, evolve, and defend them against the many distractions that could erode them.

I knew that the Short List could also work for others, so I devel-oped an app called PipelinePlus Tracker to help people focus on their most important relationships. Professional service firms around the world license our PipelinePlus software as part of their business development tech stack. After examining the behavior of thousands of users over a period of almost ten years, we noticed a pattern that reinforced the business development approach we had been teaching for years: people who pursue between nine and thirty-five relation-ships generate far more revenue and accomplish more business development activity than professionals who track more or fewer relationships in PipelinePlus Tracker. Users with fewer than nine prioritized relationships tend to have too few business development opportunities. Their close rates simply don't amount to enough new business to result in anything satisfying. Users with more than thirty-five have a hard time nurturing that many relationships. Think about regularly scheduling over three dozen lunches, meetings, follow-ups, favors, inquiries, and other personalized touchpoints on top of your existing workload and you start to get the idea.

The bottom line: PipelinePlus users who nurture nine to thirty-five relationships find their books of business increasing significantly within about twelve months. Many double the value of their client base, often resulting in millions of new dollars for their firms and meaningful remuneration for them personally.

Case in point: a global law firm came to us with a list of smart, capable partners. These lawyers had tremendous professional networks and impressive clients, but their disorganized approach and billable demands prevented them from realizing their full potential. Through regular coaching and using the PipelinePlus Tracker app to manage their Short Lists, they generated over 60 million dollars in new client business in just under two years. I cannot tell you how satisfying it was for me to see their results come in. They were pretty satisfied too.

LESS IS MORE

In the early years of a career, it is important to meet as many people as possible and establish a broad base of relationships that align to your business goals. If you're in professional services, that will likely mean focusing on the relationships that help you find the right firm and a loyal roster of clients, or book of business. If you're an entrepreneur, it will require interactions with investors, strategic partners, and prospective clients. If you're looking to change careers, you'll entertain a host of job interviews and conversations with friends who can connect you to potential employers. If you're looking to move up the corporate ladder at your current company, you'll schedule meetings with various stakeholders in your organization. This early chapter of your career is the only time when a high-volume approach to networking is important and inevitable.

But later, as we become more established and adopt greater personal and professional responsibilities, we discover that the only way to triage our time is to adopt the principle of "less is more." We become discerning about the commitments we make, the events we attend, and the groups we join. Similarly, we need to narrow our network into a cohort of select people who can grant quicker access to bigger opportunities.

YOUR NETWORKING STRATEGY EVOLVES OVER TIME

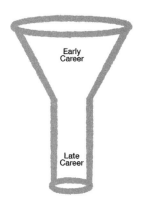

Early Career

Late Career

Those who do not develop a more focused pipeline often get stuck at a mid-level professional plateau. Their contribution to their firm remains limited to whatever is delegated to them by their managers or senior partners, and they achieve only the success afforded by their technical proficiency and the few influential relationships they've developed through happenstance. Most of their control over the direction of their careers is lost, and they are far less likely to grow into true business leaders. Similarly, entrepreneurs with mediocre networks find they cannot break through to the next level of success because they can't get into the board rooms where those decisions are being made.

When they begin to think about why their careers stalled out, they conclude that their workloads didn't leave any time for business development. Their first instinct may be to pin the blame on circumstances beyond their control, but in most cases their outcomes are a byproduct of a neglected Short List.

It typically takes about twenty years for highly effective people to build a broad professional network, and then to winnow their long list of connections down to the key power players who can shape a successful career. The reason for this is the long sales cycle in B2B professional services. When you're selling a relationship as a trusted advisor, first you need to build a solid reputation in your industry (which can take years), then you need to earn the trust of prospective buyers and stay top of mind until they are ready to hire you (which can also take years). The principles in this book will enable you to accomplish your career ambitions in a fraction of that time.

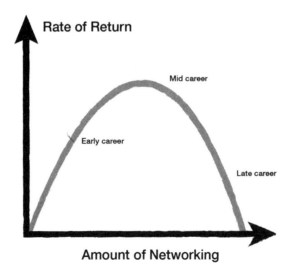

EFFICIENCY CREATES VALUE

It may feel cold-hearted and mercenary to eliminate people from your circle and arrange others in order of priority. But as you think through the Short List process, you'll see that there's nothing wrong with focusing on relationships that return value for value. You'll discover that when you stop wasting your precious time, you will also stop wasting other people's time. You can certainly choose to stay in touch with people who aren't on your Short List, but your expectations of them will be more social than professional.

You will discover that a well-constructed Short List is the doorway to new clients, ideas, advice, resources, job offers, promotions, investors, and introductions that make up the business results you want. It connects you to the power brokers and decision-makers who can help you to achieve your next professional goal. It ensures that your business development energy is more focused and efficient. It also makes networking more enjoyable. After all, reconnecting with people you already know and appreciate is much easier than cold calling a stranger.

But you'll only get there if you clear space. If you're anything like me, your life is already full of things to do. It's difficult to take on a new approach, or increase your investment in new relationships, unless you make room for it. That's why, sometimes, less is more. Pare back the energy you spend on the people you don't need, so you have energy for the few people who can make the impact you want.

Exercise: Assess Your Network

 **1 minute**

Choose the statement that best describes your current state.

1. My professional network is too small—I don't have enough connections, and I don't have access to the opportunities I need.

2. My professional network is too large—I know many people superficially, but I don't have meaningful relationships with them.

3. My professional network is just the right size, composed of influential people I like and trust. I don't know what to do with them.

If you selected #1: You'll need to expand your network. In several upcoming chapters, I provide specific ways to do that. The key is to engage in activities that align with your passions, play to your strengths, and provide access to quality people. Stay tuned for specific tactics to help you achieve this.

If you selected #2: It's time to deepen the quality of your relationships. You might be an extrovert who enjoys interacting with many people but lacks a system for prioritizing and deepening key relationships. By the end of this book, you'll have the missing piece you need.

If you selected #3: The foundation is already in place. Now, you need to learn the techniques to convert your relationships into exciting new growth opportunities. You'll discover how to do this in the upcoming chapters!

Chapter 2

Knowing What You Want

During my transition from actor to business coach, I held jobs at various firms in marketing, operations, and business development departments. I observed firsthand how management used extrinsic motivators to incentivize performance among the workers. When we performed as expected, we were offered just enough money to keep us out of the job market. When we performed exceptionally well, we were offered a bonus. When we performed poorly, we were put on performance improvement plans, and worked hard to turn things around, anxious about our job security.

This model appeals to basic human emotions of survival, greed, and fear. It's the perfect crack house for an adrenaline junkie, but it's not necessarily a win-win arrangement for all. Pull back the veil at any successful professional services firm and you'll find a highly demanding culture in which many sustain financially comfortable lifestyles and professionally rewarding careers, while a subpopulation secretly struggles with workaholism, stress, depression, and burnout. Many of the younger generations who enter these work environments resist the billable requirements standardized by their seniors and churn within a couple of years.

INTRINSIC MOTIVATORS

To understand why some people thrive in these environments and others don't, consider our intrinsic motivators: the experiences that naturally appeal to our personalities and proclivities and flood our brains with dopamine, making us feel happy.

The research in Gary Chapman and Paul White's best-selling book, *The 5 Languages of Appreciation in the Workplace*, examines how different personality types experience fulfillment at their jobs. They posit that when the reward systems in our work environments are aligned with our primary intrinsic motivator, we feel appreciated and experience career satisfaction.

Over the past ten years, we have adapted this model in our work with firms and found that of the five languages, four intrinsic motivators resonate most in professional services:

1. Monetary compensation, bonuses, and other financial incentives (Chapman and White call this "Physical Gifts").

2. Positive feedback from clients or partners, acknowledging good work ("Words of Affirmation").

3. A support system that anticipates needs, adds efficiency, and distributes workloads ("Acts of Service").

4. Attention from senior partners, including mentorship and inclusion in important projects or committees ("Quality time").

Take a moment to reflect on these four motivators. Which would you say is most important at your job: money, feedback, support, or attention? Do you have a secondary motivator among these four? If your primary intrinsic motivator is money, you will find that the traditional incentives in the corporate world are well-suited most of the time. But if receiving verbal encouragement, having a support system, or receiving meaningful attention from your managers are also important to you, you'll want to surround yourself with colleagues who also provide those experiences. Otherwise, you will eventually feel undervalued, and the financial incentives in your compensation package will deliver diminishing emotional returns.

IDENTIFYING YOUR PROFESSIONAL GOALS

After reflecting on the work environment that motivates you (the why), focus on the professional goals you want to achieve there (the what). A clear goal will help drive any successful endeavor.

Professionals with vaguely defined goals tend to be only vaguely successful. They set up business development meetings with their professional contacts, and eventually, their efforts bear fruit. Sort of. Perhaps they get a client, not necessarily the ideal client, but certainly better than nothing. Perhaps their prospective employer offers them a new job, not necessarily the job of their dreams, but better than the one they have. Perhaps the prospective investor agrees to contribute to their startup, not at the terms they'd prefer, but . . . you get the point.

If they had gone into the process with clearer goals, they might have known what to ask for when they met with their contacts, including introductions to the people who could get them what they actually wanted. And if they didn't have access to those people, they would start getting creative by joining the organizations that could expose them to their ideal prospects. Instead, they settled for whatever was available.

A few years (and compromises) later, they have a book of business made up of suboptimal clients, or a resume that doesn't reflect the career trajectory they feel they deserved, or a gaggle of small investors who can't properly fund their company. I'm not suggesting that being opportunistic is bad, only that being strategic is better. And when it comes to your Short List, having specific goals will pay off in the long run.

YOU'RE SMART. BUT ARE YOUR GOALS SMART?

Begin by asking yourself what outcomes you want to accomplish over the next twelve months. Apply a SMART framework to your goalsetting so your goals are Specific, Measurable, Actionable, Realistic, and Time-Bound. Precise descriptions will help to focus your actions. An undefined goal like "get a better job" will not provide a clear sense of direction. A SMART version of this goal might be: "get a new job at a national firm by the end of summer that pays at least 15 percent more than I'm currently earning, with the potential for advancement within the next two years, working with a team of people I enjoy."

Let's break this goal down into its **SMART** elements:

> **Specific:** "Get a new job at a national firm . . . working with a team of people I enjoy." These descriptors ensure that the outcome is guided by a distinct set of positive circumstances. You'll narrow your focus to larger firms, and you'll look for the kind of culture and team dynamic that fits your vision.

Measurable: ". . . pays at least 15 percent more than I'm currently earning." You know how much you're earning now. Add 15 percent and you've got your new salary. You will negotiate your compensation much more confidently with a clear number in mind.

Actionable: You can act on this goal by updating your resume, submitting it to prospective employers, and networking with a Short List.

Realistic: Certainly, it is realistic to expect an increase in compensation and the opportunity to work on more interesting projects within a two-year time-frame at most firms.

Time-Bound: "Get a new job . . . by the end of summer . . ." This deadline puts some healthy pressure on your job search. If you get to the end of spring and you still haven't started the process, you will be less likely to continue procrastinating.

YOUR SMART GOALS INFORM YOUR SHORT LIST.

Once the goal is clearly defined, you can start thinking about the Short List that will help you achieve it. The people on your list might include:

- Friends who work at national firms. (They can make helpful introductions and suggestions on how to navigate their environments.)

- Decision-makers at national firms. (They can either consider you for open positions or introduce you to the right people in their organizations.)

- Recruiters in the industry. (These professional connectors make it their business to know of career-advancing opportunities. They can also provide helpful advice to jobseekers.)

- HR professionals. (These people recruit, screen, interview, and place job applicants. They can also be good sources of information for anyone looking to make a move in your industry.)

- Service providers who serve clients in the space. (They often have relationships with gatekeepers and decision-makers.)

- Career coaches. (They can keep you on track, provide advice, and occasionally, make introductions.)

A quick LinkedIn search will likely reveal these kinds of people in your network. (Simply type the name of a national firm where you'd like to work, and LinkedIn will tell you how many of your first-tier connections currently work there or have worked there in the past. I'll discuss LinkedIn more in chapter eight.) If you need more inroads, search your favorite podcast platform for programs and episodes that feature the firms and profiles you have in mind. Add the interviewers, interviewees, and hosts you resonate with most to your Short List, even if you don't have a relationship with them yet. In future chapters, you'll learn how to establish a connection with anyone, even a stranger, so you can develop a relationship and start helping each other.

You can create SMART goals for your book of business, your professional development, the committees you belong to, even for specific clients, but to avoid overwhelming yourself, it's best to limit your focus to two-to-three professional objectives at any given time.

In *The Four Disciplines of Execution*, McChesney, Covey, and Huling show that when businesses focus on two-to-three goals, they often achieve them. Yet, when those businesses try to tackle four or more goals, they are less successful, only completing one-to-two of them. That's because it takes considerable energy to pursue a SMART goal, whether you achieve it or not. The theme of "less is more" applies to your objectives too.

Here are a few more examples of SMART goals you might set for yourself, and the Short Lists that can bring them to fruition:

> SMART Goal: Increase my book of business by 25 percent over the next twelve months.

Short List candidates:

- Existing clients (Let your most enthusiastic clients know that you're ready to take on more work. They may either send you new projects or introduce you to other prospective buyers in their networks.)

- Prospective clients (If your book of business is growing too slowly, you'll need to increase the number of prospects in your Short List.)

- Referral sources (These connectors can be a productive source of new business when properly incentivized, so make sure you are looking out for their interests too.)

> SMART Goal: Get a promotion within the next six months that includes a pay increase of at least 10 percent over what I'm currently earning.

Short List candidates might include:

- The decision-makers who can promote you.

- The mentors and sponsors who can champion your cause.

- The head of HR so you can find out what advancement opportunities are available, and what it would take to secure them.

- A recruiter to find alternatives you can use for leverage (or change companies if it doesn't work out).

- Your direct manager (assuming it isn't their job you're gunning for).

- A career coach who understands salary negotiations so you can get the compensation package you deserve.

> SMART Goal: Raise $500,000 for my startup business by the end of the year.

Short List candidates might include:

- Potential investors.

- Fellow startup owners (they can introduce you to their investors, or give you pointers on how they raised money for their businesses).

- Potential customers (the revenue you secure from them gets you closer to your goal, and their testimonials and case studies can help you tell a success story to potential investors).

Once your SMART goals are in place, every move you make should align with and advance your progress toward the resulting outcomes. This gives your actions focus and purpose, cutting through the destructive self-talk that might occasionally occupy your thoughts. Remember, without your own goals in the mix, your days will consist strictly of the execution of other people's goals. A recipe for eventual dissatisfaction. It's not anyone else's job to take care of your personal and professional fulfillment. While SMART goals don't guarantee success, they help you to be more precise in your vision and proactive in your pursuits. That way, your results have a better chance of reflecting the outcomes you deserve.

Exercise: Define Your SMART Goals

 5–15 minutes

Step 1: Crystalize Your First SMART Goal

Referencing the previous examples and the following SMART Goals Worksheet, flesh out one of the SMART goals you want to accomplish over the next twelve months. Make sure it is Specific, Measurable, Actionable, Realistic, and Time-Bound, because you're smart enough to know that when it comes to goalsetting, a shortcut can easily lead to a dead end.

Step 2: Rinse and Repeat

Once you've clarified your first SMART goal, repeat the exercise for your second and third goal. Use the QR code to download a clean PDF copy of the SMART Goals Worksheet if that helps you think through the process.

SMART Goals Worksheet

Describe your goal, at a high level: _____ _____		
Now, let's make it SMART		
S	Specific: Describe the outcome in detail. What are 3 conditions for success?	[] _____ _____ [] _____ _____ [] _____ _____
M	Measurable: Use units of measurement to describe success such as money (how much), timeframe (how fast), or outcomes (how many).	[] _____ _____ [] _____ _____ [] _____ _____
A	Actionable: Is this a goal you can proactively pursue? If so, it's actionable. If it's mostly beyond your control, you'll have little agency to advance it.	[] **YES** [] **NO**
R	Realistic: Is there at least a 50% chance you will be successful? If so, it's realistic.	[] **YES** [] **NO**
T	What is your time-bound deadline for completion?	**Deadline:**
Now, combine these elements and describe your SMART goal. _____ _____ _____		

Chapter 3

The Three Relationship Categories on Your Short List

Now that you are clear on where you want to go, you can start thinking about the Short List of people who can help you get there. Because not everyone on your contact list will turn out to be a good candidate for your Short List, the next few chapters will provide a systematic method to determine who stays and who goes.

The names on your Short List will fall into three categories: clients, prospects, and connectors. Some may qualify for more than one bucket, so think about the role that describes their most likely contribution and organize them into the category that describes them best.

CLIENTS

Clients recognize your value and pay for it. Depending on the kind of work you do, they are your employer, investor, or an existing consumer of your services. They fortify your existing business with greater profit and stability.

As their service provider, your clients are your first priority. Taking care of their current and future needs is foundational to the health of your business. After all, it is far easier to acquire an additional piece of work from an existing client than to pick up a new piece of work from someone you've never met. Your clients already know you and have firsthand experience of your capabilities, which is why it's likely that they will hire you again.

Clients come in three subcategories based on the current and future value they represent to you and your firm.

- High-value clients generate a sizable amount of work for your firm or have the potential to. They also appreciate your work and would be likely to recommend you to a friend or colleague for an appropriate need.

- Medium-value clients generate moderate work, have moderate expansion potential, and might recommend you, but only occasionally.

- Low-value clients typically represent the lowest common denominator of quality, collectively providing a greater volume of work at a lower profit margin. They are difficult to expand and rarely offer recommendations.

LOW-VALUE Clients	MEDIUM-VALUE Clients	HIGH-VALUE Clients
Large volume of work at low profit margin	Generate a moderate amount of work	Generate a sizeable amount of work
Difficult to expand	Moderate expansion potential	Appreciate your services
Rarely offer recommendations	May recommend you to a friend or colleague	Will recommend you to a friend or colleague

Most firms have a relatively small number of high-value clients, but their combined fees represent the majority of the organization's revenue. To the extent you have your own high-value clients, dedicate your business development energy to expanding those accounts. This means investing time to understand their businesses, their industries, their competitors, and their long-term strategies. In future chapters, you will learn how to improve your ratio of high-value clients so you can grow your book of business quickly.

Your medium-value clients warrant less individualized in-person attention from you, but they should receive personalized invitations to firm-hosted events and webinars, as well as any relevant thought leadership you produce (more on this in chapter seven).

For your low-value clients, automate your outreach to them as much as possible. Include them in general firm announcements, industry alerts, holiday cards, general content, and anything else that provides a touchpoint with minimal effort.

If you are earlier in your business development journey, you may only have low-value clients. Or you may be acutely aware that, as you achieve your long-term goals, today's high-value clients will only qualify as medium-value in a few years. Try not to overthink it. Divide your clients into the three categories based on where they sit relative to each other given your current book of business. As you apply the concepts in this book, your definitions will evolve.

PROSPECTS

Prospects are in a position to engage your services or work at companies that can hire you but haven't yet. You'd like to work with them, but you still need to persuade them to do so. They represent the opportunity to expand the scope of your existing business.

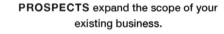
PROSPECTS expand the scope of your existing business.

Most people waste their energy pursuing anyone and everyone with a potential need for their services. And while their unfocused prospecting may occasionally bring in a new piece of business, they only realize years later that they have built an ad-hoc book of clientele that consists mostly of low-value clients.

If your prospecting is strategic and you build a book of business through a Short List oriented around high-value targets, you will find that your prospecting energy pays off nicely. You will secure exciting work with people who appreciate you, recommend you to others, and compensate you generously.

CONNECTORS

Connectors bring you new ideas, referrals, resources, clients, or other business opportunities. They may be partners at your firm or external referral sources providing adjacent services to your industry. Some connectors take the guise of a mentor or sponsor, championing your career success and granting access to influential networks. Others offer fresh ideas that can transform your thinking.

CONNECTORS expand your business with new relationships, ideas, and opportunities.

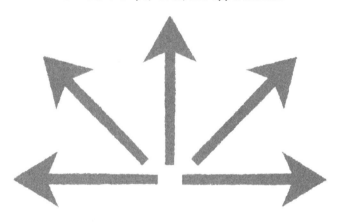

The term "connectors" originated from Stanley Milgram's Small World Experiment, which he conducted during his time at Harvard University in the 1960s. Milgram sent several packages to random people living in Omaha, Nebraska, asking them to forward that package to anyone who they thought could bring it closer to its addressee, a stranger in Boston, Massachusetts. He found that, on average, it took six transactions before the package reached its Boston recipient. This is where we got the phrase "six degrees of separation." In his book *The Tipping Point*, Malcolm Gladwell expands on the "small world" principle. He posits that each of these degrees of separation shared the same trait: they were connectors—people with extensive networks. His theory makes sense. If you want to get a package to someone you don't know, you might start by handing it to someone you do know, who seems to know everybody.

Connectors are often at the center of an otherwise weakly connected network. And because they have the best sense of the people who make up that community, they are excellent resources for anyone looking to find a particular kind of prospect within the network, or just beyond it.

Connectors may be community leaders, like your pastor or rabbi, with ties to the influential figures within your religious community. They may be a current mentor or former instructor, able to connect you to advice and information that can help you succeed. Or they can be a referral source within, or external to, your firm. These fellow professionals understand what you do and introduce you to prospects. They typically practice in noncompeting disciplines, and when managed well, can become long-term, consistent sources of new business. When you surround yourself with like-minded referral sources with potential access to the kinds of clients you want to work with, it's only a matter of time before you gain that access yourself.

The more you interact with the high-value clients, prospects, and connectors in your network, the more you will be exposed to interesting interactions and profitable projects.

Exercise: Creating Your Short List

 3–5 minutes

Now that you understand the three relationship categories, you're ready to build your initial Short List, focusing on the clients, prospects, and connectors who align with your SMART goals.

Clients to add:

- Your top five clients in terms of revenue.
- The client who pays the fastest. (You'll definitely want more work from them.)
- The two clients who have the greatest potential to expand their scope of work with you over the next year.
- The client you would feel most comfortable asking to be a reference.
- The client you enjoy working with the most.

Prospects to add:

- The prospect who is most likely to engage your services in the next six months.
- The prospect who most resembles the kind of client you want to be working with five years from now.
- The prospect who represents an interesting new area of work or industry opportunity.

Connectors to add:

- The connector who most recently sent you a referral.
- The connectors who helped you get the top five clients you listed previously.
- The connector you turn to most often for advice.
- The connector with the most influence in your firm.
- The connector with the most influence in your industry.

	NAME	COMPANY	CATEGORY (Client/Prospect/Connector)
1			
2			
3			
4			
5			
6			
7			
8			
9			
10			
11			
12			
13			
14			
15			
16			
17			
18			
19			
20			
21			
22			
23			
24			
25			
26			
27			
28			
29			
30			

Don't worry about the number of names on your list. Whatever you've written down is a great place to start.

Chapter 4

The Characteristics of the People on Your Short List

With your intrinsic motivator in mind, your SMART goals in place, and your most important prospects, clients, and connectors listed out, you can turn your attention to influence. To what degree can the people on your Short List advance your SMART goals?

Let's say your SMART goal is to secure more clients, but your Short List consists of a minor client, a couple of unlikely prospects, and a handful of marginally effective connectors. If they do not have the potential to become, or refer, the kind of clients you want, then their influence is too low, and their presence on your Short List will only be a distraction.

In this instance, it's better to have a sparse Short List than to pad it with unhelpful names. At least then you can seek out your next win: a person with a high influence score who accurately represents your access to a meaningful opportunity.

An influence score is a scale of one to five that helps you qualify people for your Short List. You start by putting yourself in the middle of the scale with a score of three. (At this point, you can legitimately see yourself as the center of the universe. Enjoy the moment.)

Then assign a score of one or two to the people who have less influence to drive commerce than you do, or who don't reciprocate your gestures of goodwill. Those who act as gatekeepers should get a score of four, and decision-makers get a five. For example, if you're trying to get a significant promotion at your company, your boss (who can put in a good recommendation) will be a gatekeeper in this framework with a score of four. Your boss's boss who makes the final call will be the decision-maker with a score of five.

Your Short List should include only the people to whom you assign an influence score of three or higher. That's because the more you surround yourself with people whose influence scores are equal to or higher than yours, the more exposed you will be to the kinds of deals, projects, and opportunities that drive your upward progress.

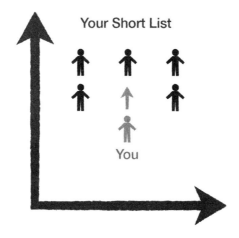

As you continue to invest more of your time interacting with the gatekeepers and decision-makers (people to whom you've assigned influence scores of four or five), your assessment of where you belong in your hierarchy will naturally rise. When that happens, you and all your fours can be reassigned a score of three. Then you'll adjust the scores of everyone else on your Short List by comparison. This will create space at the highest level, prompting you to seek out more influential decision-makers whose status aligns with your growing aspirations.

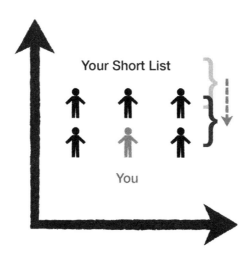

The idea here is that birds of a feather flock together. We humans are, by nature, like pack animals. We tend to gravitate toward people with the same socioeconomic conditions that we have because then we can relate to (and complain about) the same things. If I drive a beat-up Yugo and my friend drives a Porsche, there may be a sense of economic inequality in that relationship. Whereas if we both drive used, down-market cars, we can commiserate about how hard it is to afford a Porsche. Or if we both drive Porsches, we can geek out about the various features in our respective models. There may be some initial incompatibility to get over when you have an influence score of three and you're getting to know someone who's a five; less so if they're a four (unless you discover other commonalities to bond over).

This shifting of the scale keeps your Short List growing in influence as you make progress in your career. It restrains you from cluttering the list with people who no longer have the clout to accelerate your growth. As you revisit your assessment of an old friend who has always wanted the best for you but whose advice and referrals haven't panned out, or a contact with whom you have excellent chemistry but who lacks ambition, you'll reassign lower influence scores to them, or simply remove them from your list.

This approach may seem counterintuitive and a little uncomfortable at first. After all, it is only natural for us to surround ourselves with like-minded people. We feel most at home when our communities reflect similar mindsets, interests, ambitions, and life experiences. Such environments engender feelings of trust and safety, even a sense of belonging. But they rarely produce opportunities that take us to new heights or challenge us to become greater versions of ourselves. Instead, they tend to reinforce fixed behaviors.

In a joint psychology study from Wellesley College and Kansas University, researchers compared friends and partners who shared many similarities at the outset of their relationship to those who did not initially share the same demographics, values, and perspectives. The study found that relationships in the former category reinforced the behaviors that had been in place when the parties first met, whereas relationships in the latter category were much more likely to influence changes in each other over time.[5]

So, by exposing ourselves to people who reflect our vision of who we want to be in the future, we naturally start to adapt to their mindsets, interests, and ambitions; and before long, we find ourselves engaged in conversations that open a new world of possibilities.

THE FOUR CHARACTERISTICS OF SUSTAINABLE PROFESSIONAL RELATIONSHIPS

You may have heard the phrase that people come into your life for a reason. If you reflect on your past, you'll find that the reason most of the people you encountered were there was to fulfill a short-term need and solve a problem before they moved on. A smaller number of people stayed in your life for a few months or years, usually tied to a job or project, and when it concluded, you fell out of touch. Then there were those rare relationships you sustained for decades because they were meaningful enough to warrant the effort it took to nurture them. In a business context, sustainable, long-term relationships must have four characteristics: positive chemistry, meaningful character, the right level of capability, and a spirit of collaboration.

---

5   Brendan M. Lynch, "Study Finds Our Desire for 'Like-Minded Others' Is Hard-Wired," *KU News*, February 23, 2016, https://news.ku.edu/news/article/2016/02/19/new-study-finds-our-desire-minded-others-hard-wired-controls-friend-and-partner.

Chemistry

Chemistry is paramount to a sustainable relationship. It's nearly impossible to nurture connections with people whose company you don't enjoy. Very few of the people on your Short List will be your best friends, but they must at least share enough of a rapport with you to warrant an authentic, extended, mutually rewarding relationship.

Chemistry Indicators

Most of us generally know whether we like someone within a few minutes of meeting them. So, notice how you feel during your initial encounter with them. Consider your level of enthusiasm when you reflect on them and observe how they react when they run into you. When you share a genuine affection, developing the relationship comes naturally, and it never feels like work.

Character

When you first meet someone, pay attention to the behaviors that signal their depth of character, and make sure they fit your standards. Do they represent themselves professionally, or are they prone to gossip, trash-talking their colleagues, competitors, and former employers? Perhaps you are not bothered by these minor idiosyncrasies, but keep in mind that their behavior with you is not the exception to the rule. You have to wonder what they're saying about you when you're not in the room. Can you confidently refer a client to them? Can you trust that they will be there for you when you need them to be? I learned the hard way that how a person does anything reflects how they do everything. Whenever I ignored the early warning signs of poor character, I always eventually wished I had paid closer attention to the little things. So keep a keen eye on their actions, and give priority to the people who earn your respect and whose mindset is aligned with yours.

Character Indicators

If you don't yet have a sense of someone's character, pay close attention to whether they keep their word. If the meeting starts at 1pm, and they roll in at 1:10, with no advanced notice that they were running late and no acknowledgment of the time they wasted, they are telling you that they don't take the implied agreement of a start time seriously. It's worth asking yourself where else they might be casual with their agreements. When they say they will follow up the next day, do they? Or will it be crickets until you check in a few weeks later, only to receive a text that says: "OMG, I've been crazy busy" with no effort to repair the broken agreement.

Don't put that person on your Short List. Also, don't be that person. You demonstrate *your* strength of character when you are reliable, and your actions are consistent with your word. Be exceptionally dependable, so that the influential people on your Short List can trust you with the important introductions, clients, projects, and responsibilities that help you fulfill your SMART goals.

Capability

The people on your Short List are part of the professional brand you message to the world. As you affiliate yourself with a reputable firm, knowledgeable colleagues, sophisticated prospects, and powerful connectors, you become defined by the company you keep. If you are surrounded by capable people, it's easy to collaborate and refer your clients to them. Conversely, if you harbor concerns about their expertise or bandwidth, it will be difficult to send them business opportunities, or follow their advice with any confidence.

There's a great story from the music industry that illustrates how David Lee Roth assessed the capabilities at each local venue when he was touring as the lead singer for Van Halen in the '80s. He was known for his hedonism, irreverence, onstage antics, and eccentric demands. His concert contract stipulated that a bowl of M&M's with all the brown ones removed be placed in his dressing room. If just one brown M&M was in the bowl, Roth could cancel the show with full payment to the band. In his memoir, *Crazy from the Heat*, Roth explains the logic behind what looked to many of his critics like a ridiculous stunt.

Van Halen, the first chart-topping rock phenomenon to take their elaborate productions into smaller markets, typically arrived with nine eighteen-wheelers crammed with lights, props, and sound equipment. (The typical truck count at the time was three.) Unless the structural specifications in the band's contracts had been meticulously executed, floors and scaffolding could fail, huge lights could fall, or the speakers could blow, any one of which was potentially dangerous, even life-threatening, to the band and the audience. If Roth found brown M&M's in that bowl, the venue's attention to detail was suspect, and the show could be a disaster. So, what looked like the crazy demand of a diva was, in fact, an efficient and responsible assessment of his contractors' capabilities.

In order for your connectors to be valuable to you, they must have a high level of capability in their chosen field. Conversely, you'll want clients and prospects to either have a lower level of capability in your area of expertise (either because they lack the expertise, or the bandwidth to do the job themselves), so that your services will be consistently useful to them. When you encounter someone who seems like a good prospect but turns out to know more about your specialty area than you do, consider that they may be better suited as a connector.

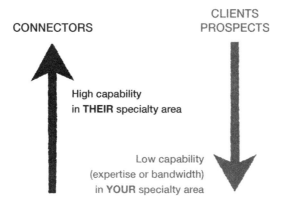

Capability Indicators

I strongly suggest that you DO NOT demand that people procure a bowl of M&M's so you can assess whether they have sufficient capability for your Short List. Instead, ask them questions about how they go about solving problems in their given area of expertise. Present them with a situation and inquire how they would apply their skills. If your contact is an accountant, you might mention a problem one of your clients had with the IRS and ask what guidance *they* would have offered. Ask the investor about their long-term strategy, and how they work with the CEOs in their portfolio. If your contact is a prospect with an employment issue, ask them how they have handled such issues in the past, or which strategies they have already applied before you offer your (hopefully superior) suggestion. If they are already familiar with your suggested strategy, ask them why they haven't implemented it. "We've just been too busy" is a great indicator that they lack the bench strength, and therefore the capability, to do this themselves.

Collaboration

There's no denying that the planet is populated by more than a few self-absorbed people. They should only hold a spot on your Short List if you can position your success as directly beneficial to them.

Ideally, you'll focus on people who understand the importance of reciprocity and demonstrate a willingness to contribute value to you. This will be especially critical of your connectors, from whom you'll expect advice, referrals, and introductions. It also applies to your prospects. If they are unresponsive or unwilling to engage with you; if they take your work sample and just forward it to their current provider instead of giving you a chance to win their work, they are not collaborative in their role as buyers. It's best to find someone else to sell to. Your top clients also need to be collaborative. You'll need them to be communicative during projects and afterwards, timely in their payments, and willing to provide references, testimonials, and repeat business. If they don't demonstrate these characteristics, you should try to replace them with high-value clients worth keeping.

Collaboration Indicators

To determine someone's potential to contribute to the relationship, look for reciprocity cues during your initial interactions. Do they ask you how they can help you, or do they only seem interested in what you can do for them? When you first exchange contact information with them, do they appear enthusiastic? Send them a helpful article or resource and see how they respond. Do they bother to thank you? Do they try to send something of equal or greater value in return? These are good indicators of their propensity to collaborate in the relationship. Surround yourself with givers (or at least matchers), and eliminate the takers, so that your good deeds are reciprocated.

These four indicators are the key to efficiently sourcing contacts for your Short List. Ask a few smart questions in your initial conversations and you will get a good sense of chemistry. Observe their behaviors and you'll start to understand their character. If you wish to explore further, propose a meeting over lunch or coffee to test their capability and observe their propensity for collaboration. Once you put this process in place, you can vet a new introduction in one or two interactions. If you skip this step, your network will be cluttered with high-maintenance clients, dismissive prospects, unsupportive managers, reluctant mentors, or passive referral sources who have access to viable opportunities but never send them your way.

A skeptic might argue that it simply isn't possible to evaluate the business potential of a new relationship in such a short time. Don't underestimate your intuition. If you think back on any failed relationship, personal or professional, there was probably something that they said or did that didn't sit well with you long before you parted ways. You may have chosen to ignore it at the time, but on reflection you can usually recall a hint that indicated something was amiss.

Example: Using Indicators to Identify a Connector

Setting: An awareness-raising event for a local charity organization.

The person at the registration table welcomes you and hands you a name badge. They also give you a drink ticket and encourage you to head over to the bar for a cocktail. You enter the parlor. There are about seventy professionals in attendance. The wait staff weave between them, offering appetizers on silver trays. You don't see anyone you recognize immediately but people are still arriving, so you make your way to the bar where a queue of a dozen people are waiting their turn to order. The person in line ahead of you (Bill, according to his name tag) notices you and nods politely. You smile and introduce yourself.

Bill: Nice to meet you. Bill Meyers.

You: What do you do, Bill?

Bill: I'm the managing partner at Libretto Advisors.

continued

You: I've heard good things about Libretto. Your firm provides strategic consulting to the Healthcare industry, right?

Bill: That's right. And you're at . . . (reading your name badge) Tyler Putnam Lewis. I certainly know your law firm. What's your specialty?

You: Healthcare litigation. I mostly work with large hospitals in the region.

Bill: I see. We probably know a lot of the same people.

You: I'm sure that's right. What brings you to this event?

Bill: (smiling) I chair the programming committee for this charity, so I kind of had to be here.

You: Couldn't send a proxy, eh?

Bill: Wouldn't look good. What can I say, volunteering is a labor of love.

You: Well, congratulations. Looks like there's going to be a great turn-out tonight.

The bartender asks Bill what he would like to drink, which gives you a moment to reflect on your interaction and Bill's potential for your Short List. He is a board member, so his influence score is at least a 4 in the context of this charity event. That's a good sign. Like you, he volunteers his time for a good cause, which suggests that your standards for character could align nicely. You also seem to share good chemistry. He is the managing partner at a reputable firm in your sector, which means he could become a valuable connector on your Short List. As managing partner, he's probably highly capable, but it would be a good idea to meet one-on-one so you can ask his advice on a topic or two and confirm assumptions. Also, you still need to assess his potential for collaboration.

Just then, Bill turns to you and tells you to keep your drink ticket. He has instructed the bartender to pour you a free drink—it's nice to see that he has the makings of a giver.

You: Thanks for the drink, Bill. I've really enjoyed meeting you. Let's exchange information and get together for lunch in the coming weeks to talk about how we might be able to help each other. Given the overlap in our healthcare network . . .

Bill: Great idea.

A few weeks later, you and Bill meet for lunch. Bill continues to impress you. He provides the kind of advice you would expect from a capable referral source. He demonstrates his propensity for collaboration when he offers to introduce you to one of the other people on the board, whose needs are a good fit for your law practice.

At this point, Bill has earned a place on your Short List. Add him to your tracking system, stay in regular contact, and do everything you can to help him reach his goals.

Note that, in this case, the assessment process only required a brief initial conversation with Bill, followed by a lunch. When you use the Short List criteria to guide your professional interactions, you become much more efficient in your ability to qualify or rule out candidates for your professional network.

Exercise: Calendar Review

 1–2 minutes

Look over the meetings in your calendar from last month. Do you have positive chemistry with the people you see there? Do you respect (or enhance) their capabilities? Finally, would you describe your relationships with them as collaborative? If so, you are spending time with people contributing to your long-term success. You're probably enjoying the process quite a bit, too.

If not, consider that you may be running in place or even losing ground. Most of your career trajectory will be shaped by the caliber of the people you spend your time with. A calendar review is a quick litmus test on this point and a reminder to start setting up meetings with more supportive people next month. If your calendar is too full to add new names, it's time to pare back on some of your commitments. You have a finite amount of time and bandwidth. Use it wisely to advance your goals.

Chapter 5

How to Refine and Manage Your Short List

As your networks grow, your goals become more ambitious, and your pattern of thinking becomes more expansive, the makeup of your Short List will begin to change. On any given day, a well-maintained Short List will be a snapshot of your most valuable current relationships. You might meet someone extraordinary tomorrow and add that person to your list. People who are now on your list will drop off for one reason or another. Their business focus may change. They may move to a distant city, become a competitor, or even fall from grace. You know that you are maintaining your network mindfully when your Short List continuously evolves over time. This approach ensures that your business agenda is reserved for those whom you have determined to have meaningful business potential.

CREATING INTENTIONAL NETWORKS

MIT Sloan conducted a study on hundreds of executives and prompted them to consult people who they had not been in contact with for three years or more. They found that the advice executives received was as useful or more useful than the advice they were getting from their current network.[6]

In a similar study conducted five years later, MIT found that the average executive tended to reconnect with dormant ties who didn't yield optimal results, favoring people who they viewed as less intimidating and more familiar, rather than seeking out people who might wield more influence.[7]

This points to the idea that we need to be intentional in creating our networks. What feels easy and comfortable will not ultimately push us outside our comfort zone or generate extraordinary opportunities.

Bursts of Value

Ever wonder what happened to that friend you knew in college and have completely fallen out of touch with? Well, here's what happened to them. They went off to start a company, sold it, became an executive at a bigger company, traveled to France and developed all these cool connections and expertise, and now they maintain a portfolio of startups across the globe with myriad service needs. Since

6   David Z. Levin, Jorge Walter, J. Keith Murnighan, "The Power of *Reconnection* —How Dormant Ties Can Surprise You," *MIT Sloan Management Review*, March 23, 2011, https://sloanreview.mit.edu/article/the-power-of-reconnection-how-dormant-ties-can-surprise-you/.

7   Jorge Walter, Daniel Z. Levin, J. Keith Murnighan, "How to Reconnect for Maximum Impact," *MIT Sloan Management Review*, February 23, 2016, https://sloanreview.mit.edu/article/how-to-reconnect-for-maximum-impact/.

you saw them last, they've amassed a wealth of experiences, relationships, and problems that need solving.

If you reconnect with this dormant tie, it creates a huge burst of value. When you meet with them, the conversation sounds like "Oh wow, it's been so long—let's catch up! What have you been up to? Well, that's exciting. I've been working on this, and maybe there's some opportunity there."

This kind of conversation has a lot more business potential than seeing your best friend, who you just saw two weeks ago, and who hasn't accumulated very many new relationships or experiences in that time. This conversation sounds more like "Great to see you again. What have you been up to?" "Oh, you know, same old same old."

From a business perspective, that initial burst of value has already occurred with anyone you regularly see on your current Short List. You're just sustaining the relationship, getting and giving a little value with each interaction, but you've already explored the obvious opportunities with that person.

Over time, relationships are like an investment portfolio. You get a 5 to 10 percent annual return from your established connections, which adds up nicely over time. But, when you first meet with the dormant tie, you get more like a 50 percent return immediately because you're catching up on years of experience. And the relationship is already there because you were besties in college. You're not starting from scratch, gradually building rapport and trust like you would with a cold prospect.

This is why you don't want your Short List to stagnate with the same names, year over year. While there will always be a core group of regulars there, you will want to curate it with new names from time to time too so that it is diversified and dynamic. By the same token, you will periodically cull those who no longer qualify, either because your goals have changed, or because their careers have evolved in ways that make them less compatible with your goals.

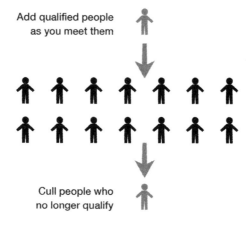

MANAGING YOUR LEADS

Given the importance of your Short List, and the dynamic adding and culling process, you'll need to be consistent about tracking. Business-minded people know the value of their bank accounts and investments. They diversify and trade assets to yield a profit and use reporting tools to track their performance. The people on their Short Lists are also assets with great profit potential and warrant the same attention to returns. Those relationships will generate the most abundant business opportunities over the course of a professional career. So, creating and maintaining a system that serves as the data collection and ROI tracking tool for your most valuable contacts makes obvious good sense.

There are a variety of resources available for keeping track of your Short List, ranging from basic spreadsheets to apps specifically designed for Short List management, to advanced CRM platforms. But our industry research shows that CRMs are mostly ineffective for pipeline management at professional services firms.

Tracking Challenges

For over a decade, we've conducted annual surveys of professional services firms to understand their evolving business development challenges. Our published research[8] consistently shows that firms struggle to use CRM systems effectively. Designed for traditional sales teams, CRMs require significant data entry and upkeep. Most seller-doers (advisors who must both sell the work and do the work) do not make the time to maintain a pipeline of client and prospect opportunities in a complex CRM system like Salesforce or Dynamics. Consider the following insights from our industry study, *The State of CRM in Professional Services*, based on a survey of over 250 US-based legal, accounting, consulting, and engineering firms.

- Nearly nine out of ten professional services firms have a CRM platform.

- Fewer than six of ten seller-doers use CRM at most professional services firms. In the legal vertical, fewer than four out of ten seller-doers use CRM.

- Only half of the seller-doers who use CRM at professional services firms use it for sales pipeline management. That translates to 20 to 30 percent adoption.

- More than half of seller-doers at professional services firms use Word documents instead of CRM for sales pipeline management.

- Seller-doers face little to no accountability for using CRM at nearly two-thirds of professional services firms.

- Fewer than 20 percent of professional services firms rate their

---

8   See: https://pipelineplus.com/the-2023-state-of-crm-in-professional-services-firms-industry-report/.

CRM as highly effective across critical marketing/business development (BD) functions.

- About one in five marketing/BD professionals at professional services firms cite their two most significant challenges as (1) low seller-doer prioritization of BD and (2) seller-doers' lack of coaching to make them effective at/accountable for BD.

Developing a Strong Tracking Method

Whether it's CRM or something else, consider the following criteria when developing your method for tracking your Short List:

1. **An intuitive layout.** Your system interface should display the people on your Short List so you can search them easily, make useful comparisons, and see right away if any of your relationship categories are underrepresented. This will help you to see clearly where your list is light on clients, prospects, or connectors.

2. **Ease-of-use.** Many well-meaning business developers invest in a sophisticated CRM product, only to discover that maintaining it is too tedious and time-consuming. Make sure the technology you choose is user-friendly enough that its complexity doesn't become a reason to neglect your list. If you're at a larger firm, don't underestimate the need for administrative support in maintaining your CRM and data stewardship for keeping a clean database.

3. **Reminder alerts.** Out of sight is out of mind. Your platform should send you a reminder from time to time if you forget to touch base with someone on your Short List. So, if you're using a static tool like an Excel spreadsheet, or worse, Word, you'll need to upgrade to a platform that reminds you to review it on a regular basis.

4. **Guidance.** Ideally, your Short List tracker prompts you with AI-generated outreach suggestions or delivers on-demand e-learning with fresh ideas on how to kindle a conversation.

We developed PipelinePlus Tracker specifically for Short List management. It has all four of the preceding criteria, as you can see from the following dashboard example with eleven people loaded into the app. Tiles turn red when outreach is overdue, yellow when outreach is required in the coming days, and green when outreach is required further into the future.

The following image shows a close-up of two Short List targets in PipelinePlus Tracker. Note that, for each person, you should have a specific task and deadline so that overdue items can be addressed right away.

Remember, the tool's effectiveness depends on the process you build around it. Your ultimate goal should be a centralized pipeline of key relationships that is consistently updated and growing. More information on PipelinePlus Tracker is included in the Appendix.

USING OUTBOUND MARKETING TO MANAGE EVERYONE ELSE

Creating and maintaining a well-designed, structured Short List is a critical business practice for everyone who is serious about accelerating their growth. But editing your contacts into a prioritized Short List does not mean that you turn your back on all your other contacts. Your approach for the masses needs to be low touch (and therefore low maintenance) but with an eye on the indicators that signal when they might be ready for more interaction. You can use outbound mass marketing techniques to stay top of mind, while reserving the more time-intensive personalized approach for your Short List.

In case you are not familiar with the term, outbound marketing is when you regularly reach out to a broad audience with information that might be of interest. While many firms invest significant sums in traditional advertising, online advertising, and PR to secure exposure through media outlets, this chapter will focus on the outbound marketing you can do yourself or delegate to your marketing team. The most common forms of insourced outbound marketing in professional services are e-newsletters, social media, thought leadership, general announcements, and invitations to events. The primary goal behind these outbound marketing initiatives is to maintain widespread awareness, but also to see who on the long list of recipients opens the message, and ideally, responds with a need for your services. While outbound marketing can be effective in reaching a broad audience quickly, it generates much lower engagement than the targeted, personalized approach you will take with your Short List.

Here are a few general rules in managing an outbound marketing strategy with your long list:

1. **List segmentation:** Categorize the contacts in your database based on industry, role, demographics, and the kinds of information that align with their interests. Segmentation ensures they will receive messages that are relevant (and not considered spam).

2. **Use marketing automation:** Automated workflows can deliver timely and relevant content based on recipient behaviors.

3. **Lead scoring:** Implement lead scoring to prioritize contacts based on their level of engagement and likelihood to engage. This alerts you to the people who are showing interest in your outreach. For example, if you have a contact who is consistently clicking on your messages about an alternative approach to financial planning, there's a good chance they are in the market for just that. Their lead score will increase in your system, bubbling them up for an invitation to a webinar or presentation on the topic. If you have an established relationship with them, they may even be ready to speak with you about your related offerings.

4. **Regularly clean and update your database:** Between career moves, retirements, and deaths, up to 30 percent of the contact information in your database can become obsolete each year. Keep the information up to date by regularly cleaning and validating contact information. There are numerous scraping technologies on the market that can do this automatically and ensure the data integrity in your database.

5. **A/B testing:** Experiment with the various elements of your outbound marketing campaigns through A/B testing. That's where you send two or more versions of the same message to see what performs better. Variations can include subject lines, content, calls-to-action, or even the colors you use in your campaigns and landing pages.

6. **Track and analyze results:** Use analytics tools to track the performance of your outbound marketing campaigns. Work toward month-over-month improvements in key metrics like open rates, click-through rates, and conversions. An analysis of your data will yield insights to help you refine your strategies.

7. **Compliance with regulations:** Ensure that your outbound marketing is in compliance with data protection and privacy regulations, such as GDPR, CCPA, or CAN-SPAM. Obtain consent before sending marketing communications and provide easy opt-out options so your domain doesn't end up on blocklists.

By implementing these best practices, you can build an effective outbound marketing strategy that nurtures the contacts in your database who are not yet prospects but could be in time. Perhaps they only rank a 1 or 2 on your influence score but will be gatekeepers soon. Or perhaps they are qualified buyers in stealth mode, consuming your content, but otherwise unresponsive. Give them time. The prospects in your long list will come forward with an interest or a need when they're ready.

Exercise: Reconnecting with Dormant Ties for a Burst of Value

 15–20 minutes

This exercise is designed to help you identify and reconnect with dormant ties—those old friends and acquaintances you've lost touch with—to generate new opportunities and value for your business and personal life.

Step 1: List Your Dormant Ties

Take a moment to think about people you used to know well but haven't spoken to in a long time. These could be college friends, former colleagues, or past business contacts. Write down at least five names.

Step 2: Research and Update

For each person on your list, do a little research to see what they've been up to. Check LinkedIn, social media, or mutual contacts for updates on their careers and current interests. Note any significant changes or achievements.

Step 3: Identify Potential Opportunities

Based on what you've learned, think about how reconnecting with each person could be mutually beneficial. What value could you offer them? What potential opportunities might arise from a renewed connection?

1. Name: _____

   Updates: _____

   Achievements:_____

   Potential Opportunities: _____

2. Name: _____

   Updates: _____

   Achievements:_____

   Potential Opportunities: _____

3. Name: _____

   Updates: _____

   Achievements:_____

   Potential Opportunities: _____

4. Name: _____

   Updates: _____

   Achievements:_____

   Potential Opportunities: _____

5. Name: _____

   Updates: _____

   Achievements:_____

   Potential Opportunities: _____

Step 4: Reach Out

Craft a friendly and sincere message to each person. Mention how you've been thinking about them, share a brief update on your own life, and express interest in catching up. Here's a template to get you started:

Hi [Name],

I hope this message finds you well. I've been thinking about you lately and wanted to reach out. I see online that you've been busy with [achievements] since we last caught up. I'd love to hear what else you've been up to.

A quick update from my side: [Share a brief update about your own life or career].

I'd love to reconnect and see if there are ways we can help each other out or just catch up like old times. Do you have some time in the next few weeks for a coffee or a call?

Looking forward to hearing from you!

Best,

[Your Name]

Step 5: Follow Up and Meet

After sending your initial message, follow up if you don't hear back within a week. When you do reconnect, approach the conversation with genuine curiosity and openness. Focus on listening and finding ways to provide value to your dormant tie.

By actively reconnecting with dormant ties, you're not only rekindling valuable relationships but also opening the door to new opportunities and bursts of value in your professional and personal life. Your Short List should include your most important connections, whether recently met or rekindled.

Scan this QR code to download a PDF of this exercise and the corresponding worksheet.

PART 2

Attracting People to Your Short List

Chapter 6

Your Niche

Wouldn't it be great if there was a special magnet that attracted high-value clients, prospects, and connectors to your business? You could just strap it to your head, sit back, and field requests from the many influential people pining for the privilege of your time and attention. Unfortunately, I am not aware of any such headpiece, but there is something more fashionable that can eventually mirror its effects: your brand.

The word brand is typically used in the consumer goods context. "That's a name brand," or "I recognize that brand." The same is true of individuals. Ever heard of Tom Cruise, Donald Trump, or Oprah Winfrey? They all have strong brands, reputations they've developed over several decades. You know what to expect from each of them, based on their past actions and accomplishments. They have built their careers around a few central themes—their niche, if you will—leveraging their personas, talents, skills, and unique abilities.

You too have a brand, even if it's only within your firm or local business community. The secret to attracting the kinds of people and opportunities that fulfill your SMART goals is to develop a brand that communicates value to the communities you want to do business with. You start by carving out a unique niche that differentiates you from your competition, then use thought leadership, effective presentations, a compelling elevator pitch, and social media to amplify your brand. But first, you must overcome the plight of the generalist.

THE PLIGHT OF THE GENERALIST

A generalist positions themselves broadly, to capture as many opportunities as possible. While there is likely a specific area where their expertise is strongest, they are reluctant to fully commit their business on that bet. Their mindset tends to sound something like this: "I can help clients from multiple industries, in myriad ways, so I should market myself accordingly and cast a wide net. After all, I don't want to turn away business." This positioning makes them the go-to for nothing specific, and they inevitably compile a jumble of low-value and medium-value clients.

Now, if you happen to be a generalist, and you are happy with your business—if it's growing at the rate you want, providing work you enjoy, and allowing sufficient time for you to relax—then perhaps you're the exception to the rule. There is something to be said for the old adage, "if it ain't broke, don't fix it." You've clearly mastered the art of multitasking, you are not bothered by a book of smaller clients, and you get a lot of satisfaction from managing a wide variety of endeavors. May you continue to thrive!

But the firms who've sought out my help over the years have

all had one thing in common: they wanted to take their business to the next level, and that usually involves an upgrade in their caliber of clientele. Sophisticated, high-value clients with complex problems and high-stakes needs can't afford to take a risk on generalists. They are willing to pay premium rates for specialists with niche expertise.

Transitioning from a general brand to a niched one isn't easy. It requires a leap of faith, but the alternative is akin to swimming upstream. Consider the many challenges that come with being a generalist:

- **Pitching:** When a prospect asks a generalist how they can help, they want a response that speaks to their specific needs. If the pitch is some version of, "I can solve just about any problem in any industry in any market sector," the prospect will be fake impressed, ask for the check, and schedule their next lunch with someone who has legitimate expertise in their industry.

- **Networking:** When their connector asks the generalist who they should introduce them to and the response is, "Just about any business decision-maker," the connector won't know where to begin.

- **Cross-selling:** The most successful collaborations are predicated on an understanding of a client's needs. This client needs help with cybersecurity. That client needs a better go-to-market strategy. When a relationship partner is considering how to expand their client team, and the client account, they will invite experts who can impress the client with their depth of expertise in the required area. They won't likely consider the generalist whose message could dilute credibility with the client.

To avoid these challenges and develop a niche that attracts high-quality work, you will need to look for the intersection of three things: your interests, your strengths, and client demand. But locating that intersection may require some reflection.

FINDING YOUR NICHE

There is wisdom in the saying, "there's riches in niches," and it is more relevant today than ever. As the business landscape becomes more complex and more crowded, it becomes nearly impossible to differentiate without a specialization. It's critical to find your niche so you can take the steps necessary to corner a defined market and concentrate your Short List accordingly. The following steps illuminate the path:

> **Your interests.** What are you passionate about? Whether it's big data or nanotechnology, AI or IT, Vegas or veganism, urbanization or climate change, fintech or FINRA, there's likely a viable market in at least one of your enthusiasms. Since it's an area of personal interest, you're more likely to invest the time and energy required to develop marketable expertise.

Your strengths. Each of us is born with unique strengths and weaknesses. Our success and job satisfaction depend on spending more time on activities where we excel and delegating or deferring those where we are merely competent. Are you a strategist or a tactician? Do you excel in vision or execution? Are you analytical or creative? Or perhaps you're a mix of both but struggle with finance? Structuring your work around your strengths will give you a competitive edge over rivals who lack your inherent abilities.

Client demand. Once you have selected an area where you have both a personal interest in the space and an opportunity to play to your strengths, confirm that there is sufficient client demand to warrant your concentration. If the partners at your firm who work in this niche are overwhelmed with work, or you are already receiving referrals and inquiries from buyers in this space, you're on the right track. But remember to look downstream too. You're better off riding the upswing of a burgeoning industry than competing in an antiquated or overcrowded sector where demand may taper off in a few years.

OWNING YOUR NICHE

Now that you've identified your niche, you'll need to take the steps necessary to establish credibility, know your competition, and build a network of industry prospects and connectors.

Your credibility. Who are the thought leaders in your chosen niche? Familiarize yourself with their books, LinkedIn posts, white papers, TED Talks, and podcasts. A credible expert in your niche will be conversant in their work. Are there any specialty certifications you should pursue to elevate your status as a niche expert? Get to know the organizations that provide these credentials.

Your competition. Who are your most successful competitors? Emulate their strengths and analyze their weaknesses. Do they have an antiquated social media strategy? Are their fees too high? Their oversight is your opportunity.

Your network. To build up the number of meaningful relationships in your chosen field, start with your Short List. Who do you know who has a connection to this niche? Take them out to lunch and see if they can help you gain access to key players. Then, call a non-competing service professional who also serves this niche. Schedule a meeting with them so you can propose an alliance where you can refer business to each other. Research organizations that serve this niche and get involved. Some examples include trade organizations, charity boards, and networking groups. Also consider LinkedIn groups and other online communities.

Your messaging. Once you have defined the sector that reflects your interests and strengths, confirmed that there is sufficient client demand for your services, established credibility, studied the competition, and taken meetings to network the niche, then set yourself apart from the generalists by messaging your business to your community. This may seem daunting, but you'll find that the sooner you educate your industry about your specialized area of expertise, the sooner they will start referring relevant business. Start by updating your bio and your LinkedIn profile so that your network is aware of your specialization, then position yourself as a thought leader in your space.

I once worked with a partner in a midsized accounting firm with a concentration in the food and beverage industry. His book of business was growing slower than he wanted, so he hired my company to coach him to greater heights. His practice aligned with his interests, but he had yet to study the space for conferences or network the niche for contacts. We made a list of the industry conferences he would attend and associations he would join. We also identified the top local service providers in the food and beverage industry. Before long, he was in contact with lawyers and consultants with the same niche. He launched an industry newsletter called the *Food Digest* to brand his business, featuring an original article and profiling a connector from his Short List in each issue. He then started an industry roundtable and invited food and beverage CFOs to attend. Many of his new connectors became valuable referral sources, just as his roundtable CFOs became new clients. Within a year, he was considered a thought leader in his niche and his became one of the fastest-growing practices at his firm.

If you are ready to transition from generalist to specialist and secure more profitable work in a niche with less competition, apply the steps in this chapter gradually over time. When people ask you what you do, emphasize the concentration in your client base. For example, you might say, "I work with a variety of middle-market companies in a range of industries, but I do have a concentration of clients in the energy sector." Over time, as you brand that concentration through thought leadership, presentations, social media, and the other tools in the upcoming chapters, you will find that the high-paying work you prefer starts making its way to your door.

Exercise: Discovering Your Niche

 15–20 minutes

Part 1: Your Interests

Take a few minutes to list activities, topics, and fields you are passionate about. Think about what excites you, what you love to talk about, and what you enjoy doing in your free time. Consider your hobbies, the subjects you read about the most, and the activities that make you lose track of time.

Examples:

- "I am fascinated by technology."
- "I like setting up sustainable systems."
- "I thrive in high-pressure situations."
- "I enjoy helping others solve problems."

Write down your answers.

_____

_____

_____

_____

_____

_____

Part 2: Your Strengths

List the skills, talents, or qualities where you excel. Consider situations where people often ask for your help, areas of expertise you have developed, and achievements you are most proud of.

Examples:

- "I can spot emerging trends."

- "I have a strong understanding of cybersecurity."

- "I am very detail oriented."

- "I can relate to people from different cultural and generational backgrounds."

Write down your answers.

_____

_____

_____

_____

_____

_____

_____

_____

Part 3. Client Demand

Research current market **trends** and demands related to your interests and strengths. Look for **gaps** in the market or areas where you can provide a **niche offering**.

Examples:

- **Trend**: There is an increasing emphasis on sustainability and ESG practices across various industries. Companies are seeking ways to improve their environmental footprint, adhere to regulatory requirements, and meet stakeholder expectations.

- **Gap**: Many businesses lack the knowledge or resources to develop and implement effective sustainability and ESG strategies.

- **Niche Offering**: Help companies assess their current practices, develop sustainability goals, and implement strategies to achieve them. This could include services such as carbon footprint analysis, sustainable supply chain management, and ESG reporting.

- **Trend**: The shift to remote work has highlighted the need for robust cybersecurity measures and efficient remote work solutions. Companies are looking for ways to secure their digital assets and optimize remote work environments.

- **Gap**: Many organizations struggle to integrate comprehensive cybersccurity strategies and effective remote work systems.

- **Niche Offering**: Specialize in remote work optimization and cybersecurity, offering services such as secure virtual private networks (VPNs), remote collaboration tools, and employee training on cybersecurity best practices.

- **Trend**: The modern workplace is increasingly diverse, with multiple generations working together, each bringing different values, communication styles, and expectations. This diversity can lead to challenges in collaboration and management.

- **Gap**: Companies often find it difficult to manage and leverage the strengths of a multigenerational workforce, leading to potential conflicts and reduced productivity.

- **Niche Offering**: Generational workplace dynamics consulting. Services include training programs on intergenerational communication, strategies for inclusive management, and workshops on leveraging the diverse strengths of different age groups to enhance team performance and workplace harmony.

Referencing these examples, name up to three niche offerings that reflect your interests, strengths, and an area where there is client demand.

1. _____
   _____
   _____

2. _____
   _____
   _____

3. _____
   _____
   _____

Chapter 7

Memorable Content

Traditionally, a person's professional reputation is a function of "time in the saddle." After a few decades of experience and a series of relevant accomplishments, they develop a brand that attracts business opportunities. But the timeline of this otherwise organic process can be accelerated through thought leadership.

DEMONSTRATING VALUE THROUGH THOUGHT LEADERSHIP

When you use content to demonstrate your thought leadership, you signal the value you can provide to the various people who either play or will play a key role in your success. Think of it as sample work product. It indicates that you can contribute informed and relevant solutions to the prospective buyers who can engage you for larger, paid projects. When you synchronize your thought leadership content with the latest market trends and the key issues that plague clients in your niche, you advance your brand in the following ways:

1. The very process of researching and producing your content enhances your knowledge base.

2. Your content can be repurposed into various formats that bolster your brand on social media and improve your search engine rankings.

3. You can share your content as a value-add with prospects as you advance them through the business development process.

Avenues for Demonstrating Thought Leadership

To share thought leadership with the world, you'll need two things: expertise and an internet connection. Then, you'll need to decide which avenue best plays to your strengths and sense of self-expression. Whether you excel at writing, thrive in dynamic conversations, or have a knack for presenting, there's a format that aligns with your natural talents and communication style.

LinkedIn Posts

LinkedIn posts are relatively easy to write and publish, and can quickly become a platform for establishing subject matter expertise among your connections and followers. LinkedIn's interactive nature encourages reactions and comments, which can lead to prospecting. (I'll cover more on that in the next chapter.)

Blogs

The content you post to your blog enhances the experience of anyone visiting your website. It acts like a comprehensive library of your thought leadership. You can easily send someone a link to one of your posts, demonstrating your expertise on the topic. Also, maintaining a blog can enhance your website's SEO, driving more organic traffic and improving your online presence.

Podcasts

Podcasts offer a more personal touch, allowing your audience to hear your insights directly from you in your own voice. Unlike other formats, they have the unique benefit of being a hybrid of marketing and business development. If you're the interviewee, you are contributing to content that can be marketed broadly. If you host a podcast, you market your brand with every episode, while interviewing prospects and clients with potential projects for your firm. The interview becomes a positive shared experience in your relationship.

Videos

Videos allow you to engage your audience through dynamic visual content. This format is ideal for those who are comfortable in front of the camera. Videos can be used to demonstrate complex ideas, share insights, and connect with your audience on a more personal level. They also enable you to showcase your personality, expertise, and unique perspective. Often after viewing a professional's video, the audience feels more connected, almost like they've met them in person.

One of the greatest strengths of videos is their versatility. You can create a wide range of content types, including informational tutorials (where you break down complex topics into digestible segments), interviews (featuring conversations with industry experts, similar to the preceding podcast concept), live streams (where you engage with your audience in real time, answering questions and providing immediate value), and case studies (where you showcase successful projects or solutions to common problems within your industry).

Note that, in order to present yourself in the best light, you will need the right camera, lighting, and video editing software (or team members who can take care of these production elements for you).

In-person presentations

Assuming that speaking is one of your talents (or at least something you are willing to work on), you should seize any opportunity to demonstrate your expertise to a group of influencers or decision-makers. But don't lecture them to death.

Certainly, it's crucial to share information that demonstrates your subject matter expertise, but too often presenters pack their presentations with facts, case studies, and takeaways, trying to show off how knowledgeable they are. The audience leaves with all the information they need, and the presenter feels like they gave away their content with nothing to show for it. Better to engage your audience, giving them just enough information so they are compelled to talk to you afterward. That should be your primary objective for every presentation: a follow-up conversation with the prospects in your audience.

At the end of your presentation, the most common reaction you will hear from attendees is, "good presentation." Your response should always be, "Thank you. What resonated most for you?" This invites them to share more specifically about the issues that are relevant to them, and possibly explore the ways you might be able to help.

Webinars

Webinars provide a more comfortable, informal forum for presentation. While it is easier to generate a webinar audience, you may not have the same level of attention as you would from an in-person presentation. Even so, webinars are a convenient and time-efficient way to take the stage without ever leaving your desk.

I am a strong proponent of webinars. I use them regularly to amplify my brand and build my Short List. One in particular was instrumental in getting my career off the ground. Soon after starting our company, my business partner and I decided to concentrate on the legal industry. Looking to establish my professional brand and build my Short List, I reflected on a technique used often in the film business.

Hollywood studios create anticipation through casting. Audiences were curious to see *Heat* when Warner Bros. announced that legends Al Pacino and Robert DeNiro would act opposite each other for the first time. *Interview with a Vampire* paired A-list leads Tom Cruise and Brad Pitt. Marvel's *Avengers* (and its many sequels) brought several popular superhero characters together. Each of these movies was commercially successful. They also boosted the careers of their supporting cast, a notable byproduct I decided to apply to my consulting career as I tackled the legal vertical.

After researching, I discovered that two of the most well-known business development consultants at the time were Bill Flannery (specializing in mid-to-large law firms) and Larry Bodine (with a niche in smaller law firms), but they had never presented a program together. I contacted them and proposed that I moderate a webinar featuring the two of them in a rare collaboration. They were intrigued by the idea of co-presenting and agreed to participate.

The webinar was a tremendous success. Larry and Bill marketed it to their respective contact lists (which dwarfed my own at the time), and firms across the industry attended the unique webinar featuring two top thought leaders. While their expertise took center stage, my affiliation with the program shed a positive light on my brand, leading to several new speaking opportunities in the following weeks. Most importantly, it introduced me to Larry and Bill, who became friends, mentors, and valuable connectors on my Short List.

Articles

Very few formats boost your credibility or penetrate the cold market like earned media. Most firms work with PR professionals to secure such opportunities, but many media outlets will entertain a pitch from the author if the content is compelling. Also, consider op-eds. Opinion editorial articles are an underutilized way to reach newspaper and online readership, especially when responding to topics motivated by controversy, legislature, or public policy.

White Papers

Long-form content requires an investment of time to be sure, but a well-researched white paper based on a survey of your industry yields insight into your respondents' feedback and gives you an edge over any competitors with a less comprehensive or less current understanding of the issues you explore. It also enhances your credibility far more than a short-form piece, such as a blog or social media post.

Pick a Path Where You Can Shine

Choose the format that complements your strengths and interests. If you're a good writer, but short on time, try LinkedIn posts. If you shine in front of the camera and enjoy interviewing others, perhaps a video podcast is the best format for you. If you enjoy research, you may resonate most with a white paper.

Once you've selected a format, you can amplify your work by affiliating it with established people, brands, organizations, and concepts. (Ever heard of guilt by association? Same idea, but with a positive outcome.)

For example, consider co-authoring your article with an internal mentor, managing director, practice group leader, respected referral source, market thought leader, or subject-matter expert. Reference credible sources in your research, and, if appropriate, relevant trade and interest groups. Co-present your talk with a referral source who can help to expand your audience. Submit the presentation to a major industry conference. If selected for the agenda, you will have yet another positive affiliation. Think of your content as a social media tagging exercise—the more reputable affiliations you can credibly attach to your content, the more points of reference its audience will recognize, the more it will be shared by cited parties, and the more exposure it will secure beyond your immediate network.

Lastly, even in your chosen niche, there is likely a fair amount of content produced by competitors, tastemakers, and traditional outlets, so try to differentiate your work as much as possible. You can do this by serializing your content around a particular theme, integrating your unique perspective, or adding a touch of humor. Allowing your personality to shine through will help your content stand apart from AI-generated noise and give your followers a sense of who you really are.

Exercise: Identify Your Ideal Thought Leadership Format

 10–15 minutes

Step 1: Reflect on Your Skills and Preferences

Consider the following formats and think about the ones you like the best:

A. LinkedIn Posts: For those who enjoy online interactions and can commit to regular activity.

B. Blogs: For those who want to archive their thought leadership and reference it in select messages.

C. Podcasts: For those who have a good radio voice and enjoy speaking or interviewing others.

D. Videos: For those who are comfortable in front of the camera and enjoy creating engaging visual content.

E. In-Person Presentations: For those who are comfortable speaking in front of an audience.

F. Webinars: For those who prefer to present ideas in a less formal, one-to-many forum.

G. Articles: For those who want to use formal channels to reach a wider audience and boost credibility through written content.

H. White Papers: For those who enjoy in-depth research and long-form content.

Step 2: Evaluate Each Format

For each format, rate your interest level on a scale of 1 to 10, and separately, your likelihood to get started on a scale of 1 to 10. Note your ratings in the following worksheet.

THOUGHT LEADERSHIP FORUM	INTEREST LEVEL (1–10)	LIKELIHOOD TO GET STARTED (1–10)
LinkedIn Posts		
Blogs		
Podcasts		
Videos		
In-Person Presentations		
Webinars		
Articles		
White Papers		

Step 3: Plot Your Ratings on the Graph

Using the preceding worksheet, plot each format on the four-quadrant graph using the letter assigned (A-H) according to your 1-to-10 Interest Level rating along the horizontal X axes, and your 1-to-10 Likelihood to Get Started rating, along the vertical Y axes.

Example:

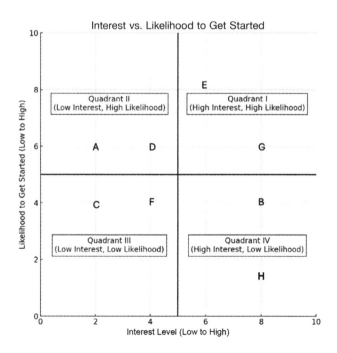

Plot your ratings:

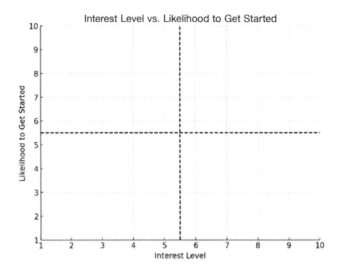

Step 4: Analyze Your Quadrants

- Quadrant I (High Interest, High Likelihood): Focus on the thought leadership in this quadrant first. These are the formats you are most passionate about and are likely to start with minimal procrastination.

- Quadrant II (Low Interest, High Likelihood): Consider these formats as secondary options. You are likely to start them, but they may not be as engaging for you.

- Quadrant III (Low Interest, Low Likelihood): Avoid these formats. They neither interest you nor are you likely to start them.

- Quadrant IV (High Interest, Low Likelihood): These formats interest you but may require extra motivation or planning to get started. Also, they may not be sustainable over time.

Step 5: Action Plan

- Primary Focus (Quadrant I): Create a simple action plan to put your optimal thought leadership formats into play. Start with the formats in Quadrant I. (For example, if blogs are in this quadrant, outline a content calendar and start writing your first post.)

- Secondary Focus (Quadrant II): Only focus on formats in Quadrant II if you have nothing in Quadrant I or if you have extra time or resources. (For example, if webinars are in this quadrant, start outlining your topic, but keep in mind the lower Interest Level rating. Consider collaborating with an experienced webinar co-presenter to make the process more engaging for yourself.)

By following this exercise, you'll be able to prioritize the thought leadership formats that align with your interests and are most likely to be initiated, helping you demonstrate your expertise more broadly.

Scan this QR code to download a PDF of this exercise and the corresponding worksheets.

Chapter 8

Memorable Conversations

Just as generating memorable content helps you amplify your brand and demonstrate value, having memorable conversations also advances your SMART goals. Whether online or offline, your interactions are branding moments, communicating the kind of professional you are and how you want to be perceived. When you have impactful dialogues that resonate with your audience, you leave a lasting impression and advance your objectives. In this chapter, we will explore strategies for cultivating engaging and authentic conversations that support your professional growth and personal character.

USING LINKEDIN TO INITIATE CONVERSATIONS

LinkedIn is an excellent forum for staying top of mind with existing relationships and initiating new ones. By sharing content and engaging with others' posts, you keep your professional network aware of your expertise and activities. But the ultimate objective on LinkedIn is to initiate conversations that you can take offline. A well-timed comment or message can transition into a virtual meeting or a business lunch, where you can build deeper connections and explore new opportunities in real time.

Of the over one billion users on LinkedIn, very few use it that way (or use it at all, for that matter). Most users are either dormant or they are sinking a lot of time into social media with little to show for it. But with the right approach, you can use LinkedIn to amplify your professional brand and nurture the relationships on your Short List in less than thirty minutes a week. While the advice in this chapter is primarily geared toward LinkedIn, most of the principles also apply to the other major social media platforms.

First, the functions:

#: Hashtags connect content to a specific topic, event, theme, or conversation. When you use a hashtag in a post, you amplify your message to anyone following that hashtag. To ensure you're following the best version of a hashtag, type it into the LinkedIn search bar and confirm that it has a strong following. For example, search LinkedIn for the hashtag that represents your industry or key interests and notice how many followers are currently listed there. If the number is at least in the thousands, click the "Follow" button at the top of the page under the hashtag name. You will now see posts in your feed that include that hashtag, so you can monitor the public conversation around the topic.

@: Mentions connect a post to a person or company. Depending on the LinkedIn user's account settings, they will receive an alert when someone tags them with a mention.

🔔: Click the bell icon on a LinkedIn user's profile to get notified whenever they post something to LinkedIn. That way, you can stay abreast of their announcements, support their posts, and stay top-of-mind. This is an easy way to stay on the radar of the important people in your network (like the folks on your Short List). If you find that the notifications are too distracting, you can customize them in the Settings menu on your profile page.

How People See Your Posts

It's important to understand that when you post something to LinkedIn, it doesn't automatically appear in the feeds of all your connections and followers. The initial audience of 1st-tier connections selected by LinkedIn is relatively small. But if that sample group interacts within the first few hours with likes, shares, and comments, LinkedIn distributes your post to a broader audience.

So, if you've ever wondered why you keep seeing the same people in your LinkedIn news feed, there are two factors at play.

1. They are among the more active LinkedIn users in your network.

2. You engaged with their posts in the past, so LinkedIn will continue to cycle their content into your feed.

LinkedIn Strategies

To excel in the game, you must know the rules. Understanding LinkedIn's functionality is the first step. Now it's time to get strategic.

Strategy 1: Follow

LinkedIn can be a powerful resource for keeping your finger on the pulse of your industry. The more you interact with other people's posts and pages, the more LinkedIn learns about your content preferences and impacts what you see in your news feed. To curate your homepage experience, follow the companies and hashtags you're interested in, mute the ones you no longer want to see, and remember to click the bell icon on your Short List profile pages. Very important (and worth mentioning twice).

Strategy 2: Connect

Social media is an efficient means of staying connected to many people at once. Make sure to invite or accept invitations from all the people in your Short List, as well as any other important relationships in your network. When you send an invitation to someone you don't know well, don't settle for the suggested default messaging. Personalize it with a sentence or two so they understand why you are reaching out. "I see you are also attending the upcoming conference in Phoenix," or "I'd like to invite you to attend our upcoming webinar on cybersecurity trends in the healthcare industry." By the same token, be discerning in who you accept into your network. If you receive an invitation from someone you don't know who doesn't provide a compelling reason for connecting, and you don't see how they could be a useful client, prospect, or connector, think twice before clicking "accept." The more your network is cluttered with irrelevant connections, the more it can dilute your feed and distract your focus.

Strategy 3: Share

Sharing content simultaneously amplifies your professional brand and provides opportunities to interact with the people in your network. When you use social media to engage with former colleagues, clients, classmates, and other connections, suspend your self-interest. If your posts solely consist of self-serving announcements like, "I'm honored to be among the few professionals selected for such-and-such award," or "I wrote this article, click here to read it," you'll pick up the occasional thumbs up or "congratulations," but people will not be likely to reshare those posts or take the time to read your article, and you'll find your engagement dwindling over time.

Seventy percent of your posts should be oriented toward helping or promoting others. You can spend the other 30 percent promoting yourself. This positions you primarily as a giver rather than a taker— a good look for your professional brand. It's also smart LinkedIn usage. By informing others, you prompt more likes, shares, and comments. LinkedIn amplifies posts that quickly accrue likes, comments, and reshares. In fact, the more quickly your post catches on with its audience, the more broadly it is distributed across your 1st-, 2nd-, and 3rd-tier networks.

Use your elevator pitch as a touchstone for the things you can share on LinkedIn. You'll learn more about your elevator pitch in an upcoming chapter, but for now, consider that your elevator pitch has four elements:

1. What you do (your niche expertise)

2. Who you help (your high-value client)

3. How you help (the problems you solve)

4. What you do in your free time (your personal interests)

Examples of Sharable Content

Here are examples of related posts you can share. Note that most of them are intended to be helpful to others, and only a few of them are strictly self-promotional:

1. What you do (your niche expertise)
   - An announcement about a niche industry event you're about to attend, with a comment about why you feel this event is worth attending. That extra sentence promotes the event and organization behind it. Make sure to add the hashtag for the event and tag the host organization so they can amplify your post.
   - The group picture you took at the industry event, tagging the people in the photo, so you are promoting them too.
   - An announcement about an upcoming talk you are scheduled to give, with a few words about what you plan to cover. That way, even if people are unable to attend, they have a sense of the topic and its relevance.
   - A few helpful reflections on an industry leader's post, with a link to their content.
   - A recap of a continuing education program you attended, and the insights you found to be most helpful.
   - An announcement about a change in job or title.
   - An industry achievement (like a top ranking or award).
     - "I'm honored to be among this year's Top Client Service Awards winners. Our industry must continue to look for ways to satisfy client expectations, especially given the myriad market pressures that challenge service standards."

2. Who you help (your high-value client)
   - A few reflections on an interesting project you're currently working on (omitting any direct reference to the name of your high-value client, of course).

- A Q&A piece, or podcast interview between you and a current client, discussing a relevant industry topic. (Make sure to get a waiver from them so you have permission to use their content.)
  - Example: "Check out our latest episode of the Market Leaders Podcast, where we interview @Don Lee on interpersonal B2B business development strategies."

3. How you help (the problems you solve)
   - A few takeaways from a recent article you wrote, or presentation you gave.
   - A few bullets summarizing the article you recently authored.
   - An excerpt from a recent webinar or podcast interview.
   - The advice you recently shared with a prospect who came to you with a typical problem (omitting names).
     - Example: "A prospect recently contacted me to discuss their supply chain challenges. Like many companies in their industry, they are struggling with labor shortages and rising expenses. We had a robust conversation about how ERP systems can streamline operations and reduce costs. I'm always happy to provide my perspective on these types of issues."

4. What you do in your free time (your personal interests)
   - A picture from the ski trip you took with your family, with a commentary on the importance of work/life balance.
   - An invitation to donate to the annual fundraiser for the charity where you sit on the board, a few words about the organization's mission, and a reflection on the satisfaction you get from volunteering.
     - Example: "I'm proud to support the annual fundraiser for @CharityOrganization. Their mission to provide education to at-risk youth is close to my heart. Join me in making a difference! [Link to donate]"

Your LinkedIn Routine

An effective and efficient LinkedIn routine shouldn't take more than thirty minutes a week. The key is to spend that time smartly for maximum impact. Avoid posting on Mondays and Fridays, as LinkedIn is most active from Tuesday to Thursday, just before and after the workday. You can schedule your posts on these optimal days, keeping your readership's time zones in mind. Of course, the more frequently you engage, the more you amplify your social media benefits, but if you're a relatively light user, start with two posts per week and advance from there.

- **Tuesday morning:** Spend ten minutes or less creating an informative post. Start with a compelling introductory sentence so your audience is motivated to read on, and tag anyone mentioned in the post so they can like, comment, and share. If the examples from the previous section aren't doing it for you, emulate the posts of successful LinkedIn users in your network. Later that morning, spend five minutes checking your notifications at the top of the LinkedIn page. It will summarize any important activity. If someone in your Short List posted something, check it out, like, and comment. If someone commented on your post, reply to that comment. If you can't think of anything substantive to say, a simple "great point" or "thanks for commenting" is enough to acknowledge their effort. Also, remember it's the number of likes and comments that counts toward the amplification of your post, not the content. Finally, send an invitation to any valuable 2nd- or 3rd-tier connections who liked and commented on your post. Your message can read, "Thanks for supporting my post today. Let's connect so we can continue the conversation."

- **Thursday morning:** Rinse and repeat Tuesday's agenda.

This twice-a-week routine, sustained over time, scales your digital brand nicely. It turns industry-aligned strangers into digital acquaintances, and it enables you to sustain and even nurture key relationships efficiently until you're ready to take the conversation offline.

SEIZING THE SIMPLE BRANDING OPPORTUNITY

Every day, on numerous occasions, you are asked some version of the question: "How are you?" "How are things going?" "How's business?" "What are you up to these days?" A generic response such as "Nothing much," or "Crazy busy," or "Same old, same old" squanders the opportunity to bolster your reputation within your network. Instead, answer with an update about a current project or an interesting client engagement. It is a much more authentic response to say, "Thanks for asking. I'm working on an interesting new project for a client in the energy sector and it's going really well." Even if the other person doesn't inquire about the details, you will have promoted your expertise, your work ethic, your enthusiasm for what you do, and your willingness to engage in a real conversation.

Try on some of these responses to "How are you?" and see which ones resonate for you:

- "Things are good. I'm working on . . ."

- "Thanks for asking. What I'm most excited about right now is . . ."

- "Well, I'd say the theme that best captures what I'm going through right now is . . ."

- "I'm doing well! This week I'm celebrating because we just accomplished . . ."

If that last example falls outside your comfort zone, you aren't alone. Unfortunately, most of the professionals I know struggle with the idea of self-promotion. They got into professional services so they could help their clients, not themselves. But their mindset overlooks the fact that modesty can be a form of inauthenticity. By downplaying their abilities, they misrepresent their potential impact. When asked, "How are things?" many start complaining about their jobs or their lives. ("Busy" is a common example.)

Why not seize the opportunity to reinforce your brand instead? Nothing boosts your professional reputation like informing your network that you contribute to successful outcomes for your clients. Promote your wins to your prospects, colleagues, and connectors so that they have a thorough sense of the company you keep, the problems you solve, and the kinds of clients you can help. Advocate for the truth about yourself: that you have significant proficiencies, and that you are just as deserving of success as your competitors.

Certainly, there is no need to exaggerate your competence, but there's no need to minimize it either. With the right mindset, any casual interaction can be an invitation to share a confident, authentic expression of your capabilities and set an example for the other person to focus on an equally empowering reply.

YOUR ELEVATOR PITCH

The term "elevator pitch" originated in Hollywood as the thirty-second summary of a movie concept. The idea is that, when you step into an elevator and find yourself standing next to someone influential who can greenlight your project, you need to be able to pitch them a compelling hook in a sentence or two before they get to their floor.

The concept applies to your introductory language in a networking context, when you are asked the question, "What do you do?" Your response should communicate your expertise in a memorable way. It's also useful if your introduction opens a dialogue so you can develop a rapport with the other person. Granted, that's a lot to ask of a sentence or two, but it's important to get it right—you'll use some version of your elevator pitch more frequently than any other conversational tool at your disposal.

When asked "What do you do?" most professionals answer with a vague, forgettable word or two, or they respond with a description that answers the question but discourages a follow-up discussion.

For example: "I'm in finance," or "I'm a lawyer," or "I head up HR at a bank" may be an accurate representation of your job, but it doesn't invite further conversation.

Instead, your elevator pitch should describe:

1. What you do (your niche expertise)
2. Who you help (your high-value client)
3. How you help (the problems you solve)
4. What you do in your free time (your personal interests)

The last element is important. You'll find that most new acquaintances can converse more easily about your personal interests, because it's the part of your life that's most relatable. Like an effective presentation, you know your elevator pitch is working when it easily flows into a follow-up conversation.

You'll use your elevator pitch when you meet a new referral

source, at mixers by way of introduction, at roundtables to make new connections, and at networking groups to introduce yourself. You may even decide to work it into your bio.

Here's an example of an elevator pitch that follows the suggested format: "I'm an environmental lawyer for large manufacturing companies. I help them clean up chemicals and garbage . . . when I'm not golfing." This one sentence successfully brands the lawyer's expertise, describes their high-value client, and how they like to spend their free time. It's a colorful way to invite a conversation about their practice, perhaps over a few rounds of golf.

There's no one-size-fits-all elevator pitch. Ideally, you'll tailor your elevator pitch for your audience, based on what you know about their background or general familiarity with what you do. While it may feel awkward at first, after a few practice runs your elevator pitch will naturally roll off your tongue. In time, you'll start to have fun with it and find that it becomes a key component in your brand.

Here's mine: "I'm David Ackert. I'm the author of *The Short List* and the CEO of PipelinePlus. We provide business development training, coaching, software, and staffing to professional services firms all over the world. And when I'm not helping my clients solve their business development problems, you'll find me burning off calories at a hip-hop class, enjoying a beach walk with my wife, reading a good fantasy novel, or hanging out with my little brother who I met through Big Brothers & Sisters of Los Angeles."

Now that you've experienced my elevator pitch, what piques your interest about me or my work? We can chat about business development, authoring, reading, technology, dancing, beach walks, or volunteering. Any of these starting points can begin a conversation that helps us build a connection.

YOUR DEPENDABILITY SPEAKS VOLUMES

When it comes to your personal brand, anyone can talk a good game, but ultimately, actions speak louder than words. People validate your claims based on the things you do and the results you produce. Unfortunately, we high achievers have a tendency to overcommit, so we must be careful that we don't become too busy to respond to emails, keep our agreements, or show up on time to our appointments, lest we erode our brand as a trustworthy professional, signaling that we may not be the best choice for that next opportunity.

Prioritize timely communication with your key relationships. You will find that doing so bolsters your self-confidence and opens the door to referrals from your network and cross-selling with colleagues. It also indicates to your clients and prospects that you are available to help. This extends even to sending a quick "thanks" by way of reply to their emails or text messages. Your acknowledgment of receipt closes the loop and ensures that they are not left wondering: "Did my advisor receive my message or did it get lost in their inbox? Do I need to resend it?" Allowing such questions to linger erodes the trust and effectiveness of your communication.

Exercise: Use Your Elevator Pitch to Drive Your Brand

 5–15 minutes

This exercise will help you craft your elevator pitch, which you can integrate into the various ways you promote yourself, including the memorable content you create, the interactions you engage in online, and the offline conversations that reinforce your brand.

Step 1: Craft Your Pitch

Use the following worksheet to craft your elevator pitch. Follow the prompts in the first three columns and fill in the column on the far right.

ELEVATOR PITCH WORKSHEET				
Elevator Pitch Component	Why It's Important	Format	Example	Your Elevator Pitch
What you do (your niche expertise)	Helps people understand your niche expertise. Satisfies their immediate curiosity about your profession.	"I'm a _____ specializing in _____"	"I'm a lawyer specializing in labor and employment."	
Who you do it for (your high-value client)	By describing your high-value client, you align your brand with the kind of work you want to attract.	"I help _____ companies…"	"I help companies with 100 or more employees…"	
How you help (the problems you solve)	The person you're speaking to may have this problem, so take the opportunity to explain it in terms that are easy to understand.	"Solve their _____ problems."	"…navigate termination, discrimination, or wage disputes."	
What you do in your spare time	This is the part of your elevator pitch that will likely lead to a conversation. Your personal interests and commitments are the most universally relatable to the people you meet.	"…and when I'm not doing that, _____"	"And when I'm not doing that, I'm usually driving my twin girls to either soccer practice or theater tryouts. One's an athlete, the other is a thespian."	

Step 2: Work Your Pitch

Once that's done, work your elevator pitch into the bio on your website, your next in-person or virtual presentation, your LinkedIn profile, and your LinkedIn posts.

Scan this QR code to download a PDF of this exercise and the corresponding worksheets.

PART 3

Growing and Nurturing Your Short List

Chapter 9

Cultivating New Relationships

N ow your contact list is edited down to the people in your life who you respect and who have the power (or at least the potential) to move your career up the ladder. They are in line with your SMART goals, they are organized into a tracking tool that's easy to manage, and they are receiving content and messaging that elevates their impression of your professional brand. But what if your Short List is shorter than you'd like?

Fortunately, between social media, social circles, social invitations, and industry socials, you can easily fill the gaps in your list. All you have to do is start networking.

Wait, did you just shudder?

Often, when people think of networking, they conjure a stuffy room full of strangers forcing small talk and exchanging business cards. But there's a better way. In this chapter, we'll help you find an approach that plays to your strengths and interests so you can connect with interesting new people with mutually beneficial opportunities who qualify for your Short List.

INTRODUCTIONS THROUGH YOUR CURRENT SHORT LIST

The people who have already made your list can help you find other people like them. A good place to start is by using the search field on LinkedIn to examine your 2nd-tier contacts. These are the people who are connected to you by only one degree of separation. Many of them may fit the profile of the people you want to meet. Focus on those who are linked to you through connections who are already on your Short List. To keep your results manageable, narrow your search by job title, industry, and geography.

When you identify someone intriguing, you already have a legitimate path to beginning a relationship. Call your shared 1st-tier connection and let them know that you are interested in being introduced. Even if they do not know the person in question, your request will likely lead to an introduction they *can* comfortably make.

Here's an example of how the LinkedIn introduction might play out: You call your former colleague Mary and say you noticed her LinkedIn connection to Hank, a decision-maker at a target company. You tell her that you do a lot of business with companies like his and would love to see if there's an opportunity to work with him. You ask if she knows Hank well enough to introduce you. Mary will likely have one of these reactions:

1. **She doesn't know Hank.** He's just a random connection in her LinkedIn network. In this case, ask Mary if she knows of decision-makers at other similar companies that she can connect you to. Then ask her if there are any introductions

you can make that would be helpful to her and search your LinkedIn network accordingly.

2. **She isn't comfortable introducing you to Hank.** She doesn't know him that well, or hasn't spoken to him in a while, or maybe she already owes him a favor and would prefer to do this at another time. In any case, ask for introductions to people who fit Hank's profile.

3. **She is comfortable introducing you to Hank.** Mary may offer to send an introductory email. That's good news, but to initiate a more meaningful start to your new relationship with Hank, consider these suggestions:

   - Offer to send Mary a blog or article you've written so she can refer to it in her email to Hank and give him a sense of your expertise.

   - If Mary and Hank are local, invite them to join you for lunch, so the two of them can catch up and you can meet Hank in person.

   - Ask if she and Hank will both be attending an event, like his company's holiday party, and if you might join her.

Ultimately, your goal should be to meet Hank in person, and preferably in Mary's company, so that she can help navigate a successful first meeting.

VOLUNTEER ORGANIZATIONS

There are those who believe that community service should be a completely selfless act and that altruism is its own reward. It certainly can be. But under the right circumstances, volunteering can also be a powerful business development strategy.

Volunteer organizations represent an opportunity to deepen relationships, contribute your unique skills, and make a difference. There are many options to choose from, including global causes, local ones, a committee at your firm, a special interest group, a non-profit organization, a trade association, or your place of worship. In the context of these groups, their leaders have a higher influence score than you do and should be considered connectors on your Short List. Not only can they include you in useful initiatives and events, but they can also keep an eye out for additional Short List candidates within their networks.

Since volunteering places additional demands on your time, it's important to be judicious. Assess each opportunity to see if these three criteria are in alignment for you: the right cause, the right role, and the right commitment.

1. **The right cause.** This is the first and most important issue. Those who volunteer strictly for selfish gain with no real interest in the cause are easy to spot in any volunteer organization. Their participation is tenuous, their tenure is short, and they often leave a bad reputation behind when they inevitably step down from the organization. So, make sure your interest in the cause is genuine. The point here is to make a difference and have fun. It's hard to do either if you're only looking out for yourself.

2. **The right role.** If you aren't careful, you can easily find yourself involved in a volunteer endeavor with no business develop-ment potential. So, make sure your role involves interaction with board members who are mostly clients, prospects, and current or potential connectors. Pursue service opportunities that serve your altruism *and* your SMART goals.

3. **The right commitment.** Boards and committees rely heavily on their volunteering members, so they will often request a significant amount of time in service of the cause. If you don't establish boundaries, you can easily find yourself overcommitted. Like your household budget, create a volunteering budget for yourself, both in terms of money and time, and communicate them to your fellow volunteers so that their expectations are established early. It might sound something like this: "I'm eager to help this worthy cause. I can commit two volunteer hours per week. As long as that is sufficient to fulfill my responsibilities, I look forward to serving the organization."

If you aren't yet involved in a volunteer activity, ask your Short List. Chances are at least one of them know of, and can even recommend, a few volunteer organizations that might be of interest. Alternatively, contact the head of your trade association, alumni organization, religious or fraternal organization, or firm committee and let them know you'd like to get more involved.

If you are currently involved in a volunteer organization that does not align well with your goals or philosophies, consider extricating yourself and re-allocating your energy elsewhere. There's no need to martyr yourself for the benefit of others. It will only lead to resentment. When you step down, you open the seat for someone who is a better fit for the organization, and you free yourself to seek a win-win opportunity that will be both personally and professionally fulfilling.

CONFERENCES

The conference industry has exploded over the past few decades. Now, even the most esoteric market sectors have at least one, if not multiple, conventions and trade shows throughout the year, gathering buyers, vendors, tastemakers, and thought leaders. Take a moment to consider the profile of your ideal client. If they are in financial services, you can populate your Short List from the next FinTech Con or Financial Services Expo attendees. If they are in SaaS, you will find prospects and connectors at conferences like SaaStr or South by Southwest (SXSW). For more examples, a Google search of the industry + "conference" will list additional options.

Pregame Preparation

Assuming you have the budget for it, it's a good idea to attend industry conferences once or twice a year. Too many professionals neglect these events unless their firms require their attendance, or the organizers have asked them to speak or included them on a panel. They don't realize that the networking alone can be worth the time and the price of admission. The key to success is to have a game plan.

Identify Your SMART Goals for the Event

Before you attend, perhaps even before you register, you should identify a measurable outcome that matches your goals for the conference. For instance, if your goal is to meet connectors in the industry, the outcome could be measured in the number of connectors you interact with at the conference. If your goal is to meet a specific person, the outcome will be defined by whether you had meaningful contact with them. If you want to use the show to broaden your network, measure the outcome in the number of business cards or LinkedIn connections you collect from new contacts. If your aim is to expand your industry knowledge, you can measure the outcome in the number of sessions you attend and the speakers you meet.

This kind of preplanning is important because it helps you define successful attendance. When you define clear outcomes, you never have to wonder whether attending a trade show was a waste of time. Either you achieved your goal or you didn't.

Form a Team

One of the best ways to position yourself for success is to "hunt in packs." Plan to attend the conference with colleagues from your firm so you can cover more ground and seize more opportunities. Or, even better, invite a client, prospect, or connector to attend with you. This win/win approach provides both of you with a "wingman" and allows you to spend an extended period developing the relationship.

Target Attendees

Contact the conference organizers for an advance list of attendees so you can identify the key targets you intend to meet at the trade show. Let them know you will also be at the conference, but don't rely on informal "see you there" messaging. Propose a specific time to meet and exchange mobile numbers. Thousands of people often attend trade shows. Without a scheduled rendezvous and a way to text each other, it is unlikely you will happen upon them.

Onsite Strategy

You've checked in at the conference and picked up your name badge. You are surrounded by a sea of strangers. How do you make the most of your time onsite?

Collect Intelligence

When you arrive, seek out the program director or programming chair. Befriend them and ask for their recommendations on sessions to attend. No one will know the ins and outs of the conference like the people who organized it. They can also help you locate the individual targets you want to meet.

Follow the event hashtag on social media to learn what and who is trending. Then, spend some time with the vendors at their booths in the exhibit hall. They will have their finger on the pulse of the event and its attendees.

Leverage Sessions

Think of the educational sessions as an opportunity to establish your presence in the room. During the Q&A, ask smart, provocative questions that communicate your interest and expertise. After the session, approach the speakers and panelists to introduce yourself and exchange business cards, then connect with them on LinkedIn. They are often the connectors and tastemakers in the industry. They may become valuable resources for you, either because of their expertise, or as co-presenters at next year's conference.

Network the Receptions

Your goal at each cocktail reception is to establish connections and identify opportunities. Use your elevator pitch to make a memorable impression, and as you get to know others in the room, note key takeaways and follow-up items in your phone or on the backs of their business cards. That way, when you return to your office, you will recall who they were and what you intended to do with them. Too often, the flurry of handshakes, conversations, LinkedIn connections, and business cards becomes difficult to track when the time comes for follow-up.

Post-Game: Follow-up

Set aside a block of time for follow-up, preferably within a day or two of the trade show. The timing is important for the following reasons:

1. The longer you wait, the more the conversations, connections, and opportunities will fade from memory.

2. Some of your competitors may also be in pursuit of the opportunities you identified.

3. Your considerable investment in the conference will amount to very little if you let your follow-ups wither on the vine.

NETWORKING ORGANIZATIONS

Networking organizations foster communities with interconnected business needs. Their primary goal is facilitating partnerships that result in client referrals and providing additional client resources. At the organizational level, firms become members of cross-border alliances such as Meritas and PrimeGlobal. On an individual basis, professionals engage with networks like ACG (Association of Corporate Growth), ProVisors, BNI (Business Network International), and industry-specific associations such as the ABA (American Bar Association), AICPA (Association of International CPAs), and SMPS (the Society for Marketing Professional Services). These affiliations serve as valuable platforms for collaboration and resource-sharing, contributing to the growth and success of both organizations and individuals. Participating in a formalized networking organization provides several advantages:

- Exposure to new connectors.

- Repeated contact so you can build relationships over time.

- A community of resources. (When one of your clients needs a service you don't provide, you can refer the appropriate contact from within the referral organization.)

Networking organizations offer social and educational events, local chapter meetings, committee involvement, and online forums. Many of them help facilitate two-way and three-way meetings so that members can get to know each other and explore synergies.

Two Examples of Networking in Action

Suzie Doran, a partner at a large California regional firm, sits on the executive committee for the OneACG global board. Her firm is also a member of PrimeGlobal. I asked her to share her thoughts about ACG, which focuses on the middle-market M&A (mergers and acquisitions) community.

> Through ACG I have access to trusted advisors in the three categories where I get most of my referral business: M&A attorneys, commercial brokers, and financial advisors. For example, I recently attended an ACG event where there was a concentration of M&A lawyers. I was able to reconnect with the ones I already knew and meet a few new ones.
>
> Whenever I meet a new potential referral source in one of the three categories, I invite them out to lunch so we can build the relationship. Assuming the comfort level is there, we exchange leads so we can grow our respective businesses.
>
> When one of my clients needs a good lawyer, commercial broker, or financial advisor, I look into my ACG network first so I can help the referral sources who helped me. It's a proactive cycle that benefits everyone involved.

I asked Matt Toledo, the CEO of Provisors, to share his perspective.

> Provisors has over ten thousand members across the US. Groups of roughly thirty members gather monthly, engaging in a process we call Know, Like, Trust, Refer. First, they get

to know each other. Over time, they come to like each other personally, then trust each other professionally. Finally, they refer business to one another. The process streamlines the relationships that form between our multidisciplinary members, made up of lawyers, bankers, accountants, consultants, and other advisors.

One of the reasons Provisors works so well is that it gives our members access to a community of helpful professionals who look out for each other, and ultimately, refer clients to each other.

Personally, much of my career success has come through other people who were willing to help me. No one gets anywhere alone. Provisors formalizes that principle for our members.

Principles for Making the Most of Networking Organizations

There are three basic principles for effective participation in networking organizations:

1. **Show up consistently.** Attend the events and make a genuine effort to participate in the meetings. Passive members are easily forgotten.

2. **Brand yourself.** Use your elevator pitch to establish a memorable introduction when you meet other members.

3. **Be generous.** Like you, people like to do business with givers, not takers, so listen for opportunities to help other members first before you expect anything to come your way.

Networking organizations can help you build up your Short List. As you meet new contacts, consider their influence scores and look for the 4Cs of chemistry, character, capabilities, and collaboration.

You will quickly establish a stable group of connectors who can help you achieve your SMART goals.

SOCIAL EVENTS

While building your Short List, accept as many social invitations as you can manage, particularly if they are extended by someone who is already on your list. You don't have to work the room or try to collect everyone's business cards. Look for people who genuinely interest you and focus on having one or two substantive conversations with them. Remember, the core theme for your Short List is quality above quantity. Here are seven networking tips for social events.

1. **Find out who will be there.** If you have a sense of the attendees in advance of the event, you can seek out those most likely to interest you.

2. **Make an appearance.** You don't have to stay for the whole thing. Aim for a few high-quality conversations. Even if you only make one or two good connections, it's worth your time.

3. **Talk to the hosts.** Seek them out, let them know what kinds of people you are looking to meet, ask them to point out a few candidates, and see if they will make an introduction or two.

4. **Eat beforehand.** You aren't there for the free food, you're there to make a good first impression and, hopefully, some good connections. Despite considerable advances in the culinary field, we still haven't figured out how to make appetizers tidy. Besides, it's hard enough to hold a drink in one hand and fish out your business card or your phone with the other. Don't further complicate the exercise by trying to balance a greasy egg roll on a

napkin or tell a joke with a mouthful of spinach dip. You don't want your first impression to be a messy one.

5. **Join groups of three or more.** It's hard to break into a conversation between two people, but if you see a group of three or more, you can ease in and join the conversation. If you need an opening line, wait for a lull and say "Excuse me, may I join you? I don't know many of the people here, so I thought I'd introduce myself." Remember, they are at the party to meet new people too.

6. **Seek out lines.** At any event, whether it's a conference or social gathering, some of the most valuable opportunities can arise while waiting in line. Whether it's the line to get food or a drink, you'll find yourself standing next to someone for several minutes with an easy excuse to strike up a conversation. And if you find that there isn't any chemistry there, you can just turn your attention back to the bartender as they prepare your cocktail.

7. **Seek out wallflowers.** You see that person standing alone in the corner, looking awkward and uncomfortable? Do them a favor and go talk to them. By breaking the ice and initiating a conversation, you can help them feel included and valued.

Perhaps you're reading this section thinking, "This is all well and good, but I don't get invited to a lot of social functions or networking events." Don't despair. Be the change you want to see in your social calendar. Look over your Short List and invite a few of those folks over for dinner. Encourage them to bring a spouse, friend, or business colleague. That second-degree connection helps expand your professional network through a trusted source.

PODCAST GUESTS

In an earlier chapter, I talked about using a podcast as a content platform to showcase your niche expertise and promote your brand. Hosting a podcast positions you as a thought leader, drawing an audience that values your insights, and giving you the perfect basis to contact and interview influential guests who might eventually find their way onto your Short List.

1. **Spotlight your Short List.** For your initial episodes, feature your ideal clients, prospects, and connectors as guests. Their presence establishes credibility for your show and provides a unique opportunity to reconnect. It also helps them by amplifying their key messages to your audience.

2. **Mine their merits.** As you interview your Short List, you will learn something new about them during each interview. After you've interviewed them, describe the kinds of guest you'd like to have in subsequent episodes and ask if they can recommend anyone from their networks. This enables you to meet the people on their Short Lists.

3. **See just where flattery will get you.** Your podcast is the perfect opener to approach gatekeepers and decision-makers in your industry. Prospects who would never respond if you reached out with a cold call will be much more inclined to speak about being a special guest on your show. After all, it's not every day they receive such a flattering invitation. The interviews establish a rapport with key players in your industry. Your follow-ups nurture the relationships into new business development opportunities.

4. **Shout, shout, let it all out.** Promote each episode on social media. Utilize relevant industry hashtags to increase

discoverability, and tag guests or collaborators to encourage them to share the content with their networks. Engage with comments to establish a personal connection with your audience. By strategically marketing your podcast, you extend your reach and create additional touchpoints for potential clients to connect with you and discover your offerings.

5. **Boost your bench.** Invite other podcasters in your field to be guests on your show. By tapping into each other's audiences, you broaden your reach and expose your brand to new potential clients. This cross-pollination can lead to referrals and partnerships, fostering business growth.

Remember, your podcast isn't just a broadcast; it's a dynamic tool for relationship-building. By weaving a narrative that resonates with your audience and strategically connecting with industry players, you transform your podcast into a potent catalyst for business development success.

ALUMNI ASSOCIATIONS

It's always interesting to discover which of your old schoolmates have advanced well in the world, and the best way to do that is to attend your alma mater's alumni events. Those who "knew you when" will vouch for you and become valuable connectors, especially if you are top of mind. Senior alumni will be more likely to hire, advise, or mentor you given your shared educational background. In some cases, staying connected to your alma mater can provide ongoing access to the faculty body, some of whom can make useful introductions for you as long as you didn't skip too many of their lectures back in the day.

PAST ASSOCIATES

As mentioned previously, dormant ties can be valuable additions to your Short List. Scroll through your forgotten emails and look at your old calendar appointments from the last five years or so. Who made up your inner circle of prospects, clients, and connectors back then? It's likely that some of them are no longer as involved in your life. Maybe they moved away. Maybe they changed companies. Or maybe you just fell out of touch for no particular reason. As a reference point, give some thought to what connected you in the first place.

As people get more mature and grow in their professions, they gain more influence and become decision-makers in their organizations, networks, and boards. Like you, they have developed a new inner circle of friends and colleagues, many of whom could also be valuable connections for you now. You don't need an excuse to reconnect. Just tell them it's been a while, you were thinking about them, and you wanted to catch up. You'll find that many of the relationships you developed in years past can yield surprising dividends today.

MASTERMINDS

The concept of a mastermind was first popularized by Napoleon Hill in his 1937 classic, *Think and Grow Rich*. He observed how people like Henry Ford and Andrew Carnegie used masterminds to accumulate knowledge, share resources, and coordinate effort. Basically, they got together on a regular basis, brainstormed, and came up with ways to collaborate. Probably over a few cigars. According to Hill, "No individual may have great power without availing himself of the Master Mind."[9]

---

9   Napoleon Hill, *Think & Grow Rich* (New York: Plume, 1990), 192.

You can use Hill's model to avail yourself too. Review your Short List and ask yourself which of these individuals would benefit from repeated contact with one another based on commonalities and business synergies. Here are a few themes to consider for a mastermind:

- **Think tank.** Invite those with an innovative mindset onto a think tank that focuses on an issue of mutual interest for the next six months.

- **Referral group.** Gather some of your connectors into a referral group who meet monthly to get better acquainted and exchange introductions.

- **Advisory board.** Form an informal advisory board where members meet quarterly to review each other's business plans and provide feedback.

A mastermind exponentially increases the benefits you gain from select individuals on your Short List. By assembling them for productive discussions, you not only contribute value to their experiences but also streamline your interactions with multiple contacts.

UNEXPECTED ENCOUNTERS

Wherever you are, you're already there. You might as well initiate conversations with the people you run into as you go through your day.

1. **Going up!** Who are all those people who file in and out of the elevator at your office building every morning? Instead of staring at the floor, or the escalating numbers blinking next to the

elevator doors, smile at the person who just pushed the button and ask them which company they're visiting on the tenth floor. With a little luck and some gregariousness, you can begin a conversation that turns a commercial neighbor into a new entry in your Short List.

2. **Taking off.** It's smart to get to know people who sit next to you on an airplane, especially when you travel in first or business class. Even if they aren't their company's CEO, they may be able to make a connection for you through their network. On a coast-to-coast flight, you'd be hard pressed to find a more captive audience, but make sure you are sensitive to their interest level in having a conversation. They may be painfully shy, or trying to get some work done, or desperately in need of a nap. Pay attention to their social cues so you can leave them in peace if they just want some me time.

3. **Workspace win.** If work takes you out of town, and you need a place to sit down and get through a project, ask a local client if you can use their guest office or conference room. Most companies with commercial space can accommodate the request, and you will inevitably get some face time with client contacts in that office. Ask them if they would like to be your guest for lunch or a cup of coffee while you're onsite so you can learn more about their local needs.

4. **Serendipitous moments.** Your mileage may vary on this strategy depending on your comfort level initiating conversations with total strangers. Mine happens to be high, so when I travel for business, I always try to put myself in surroundings that are conducive to meeting influential gatekeepers and decision-makers. Barring the preceding "workspace win" strategy, I bring

my laptop to the most upscale hotel lobby in the area and strike up conversations with the bougie guests killing time on velvet couches, sipping cappuccinos and listening to ambient electronica. When it's time for dinner, I'll seek out an upscale restaurant and order my food at the bar so I can strike up a conversation with the people around me. (My dining strategy can be summed up in two words: avoid tables.) My approach frequently puts me in conversation with people from industries that are vastly different from mine, in circumstances that don't arise within my usual orbit. These unexpected encounters wouldn't have happened otherwise and have often led to quality time with fellow executives and world travelers. It's how I met some of my Short List candidates, and even a few valued friends.

As you explore these networking forums, you will make new friends and acquaintances. Apply your prequalifying criteria. Are they a prospect, client, or connector? Do they possess the 4 Characteristics (chemistry, character, capability, collaboration) and an influence score of 3 or higher? Now that you know what to look for, you can answer these questions efficiently for yourself and round out your Short List accordingly.

Exercise: Leveraging Untapped Networking Forums

 5–8 minutes

This exercise will help you assess and activate the networking forums that are best suited to you.

Step 1: Assess Your Comfort Level

Rate your comfort level with each of the following networking forums on a scale of 1 (least comfortable) to 10 (most comfortable).

FORUM	COMFORT LEVEL (1–10)
Introductions Through Your Current Short List	
Volunteer Organizations	
Conferences	
Networking Organizations	
Podcast Guests	
Social Events	
Alumni Associations	
Past Associates	
Masterminds	
Unexpected Encounters	

Step 2: Review Your Ratings

Identify the forums where you feel most comfortable (scores 7–10) and those where you feel least comfortable (scores 1–3).

Step 3: Choose an Untapped Forum

Among the forums you rated as most comfortable (7–10), select at least one that you have explored the least. This should be an environment where you feel relatively at ease but have not yet leveraged to its full potential.

Step 4: Tap It

Look for upcoming events, groups, or activities within this forum where you can participate. For instance, if you chose "Conferences," identify a relevant industry conference you can attend in the coming months. If you chose "Podcast Guests" and you don't currently host a podcast, take an achievable step and ask to be a guest on someone else's podcast before launching your own. If you chose "Unexpected Encounters," challenge yourself to initiate friendly conversations with strangers in social environments where you feel safe and explore their potential as new connections.

Step 5: Follow Up

When you encounter new contacts in these networking forums who possess the 4Cs and a 3+ influence score, arrange a virtual (or, if possible, in person) follow-up meeting so you can qualify them for your Short List.

Scan this QR code to download a PDF of this exercise and the corresponding worksheets.

Chapter 10

Maintaining Existing Relationships

It's a good thing your Short List is, well, short. Its brevity ensures you can focus not only on activities and networking forums that add new people to it but also on the care and maintenance of those already on it. Nurturing your most valuable relationships requires intentional effort, because time is the enemy of connectedness.

While there are a few people with whom we share a special bond, where every reunion feels like no time has passed, most connections atrophy over time. We lose touch, and as time goes by, we feel increasingly awkward about checking in. We might feel guilty for neglecting the relationship, and since they haven't reached out either, we assume they have lost interest in us. But the reality is much more mundane. Anyone who is actively engaged in their professional and personal pursuits (with an influence score of 3 or higher) will struggle to keep up with all the important people in their various networks, especially if they lack a system for staying in touch.

This is why keeping a Short List is crucial. It helps you focus on a manageable number of key relationships that are worth your time and effort. But maintaining them is strictly your responsibility. After all, they are your need-to-haves.

NICE-TO-HAVE VERSUS NEED-TO-HAVE RELATIONSHIPS

At any given point in our lives, our existing relationships either fall into the "nice-to-have" or "need-to-have" category. As a child, the immediate family makes up the network of need-to-haves, providing the food, shelter, guidance, and love necessary to survive. As adults, we encounter more and more nice-to-haves.

From Casual to Sustainable Relationships

A great example of nice-to-have versus need-to-have for adults is the rocky road many of us experience when dating. When you are seeing someone casually, getting together is a nice-to-have. If they fail to respond to a text or two, you might be disappointed, but because both of you made a minimal investment in the relationship, it's easy to move on. When both people approach a relationship from a nice-to-have perspective, it tends to be short-lived. Other priorities inevitably prevail.

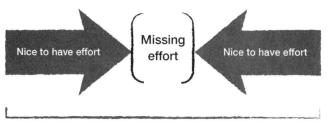

Effort required for a sustainable relationship

If the relationship gets serious and you become emotionally invested, you might make more effort, confronting the communication breakdown, asking them whether the two of you are on the same page, and establishing some ground rules with a long-term view in mind. Ideally, they will step up, stop playing the field, and realize that they need to have you in their lives. When both parties have a need-to-have mindset, there is overlapping effort, and you have a fighting chance of working through the many issues you'll have to confront as a couple, like their overprotective mother and that jealous ex who keeps calling at odd hours.

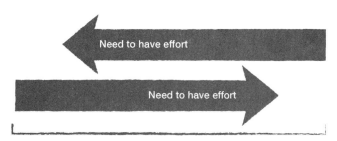

Effort required for a sustainable relationship

Your Short List consists of people you've decided you need to have in your life to achieve your professional goals. As you establish these relationships, unless you quickly find your way onto *their* Short Lists, they will not be as invested in you as you are in them. They will consider you a nice-to-have and make significantly less effort to stay in touch. That doesn't mean they won't be happy to hear from you, but you will be the one initiating contact for the most part.

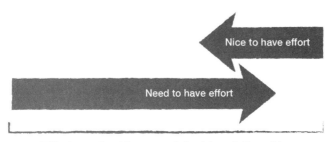

Effort required for a sustainable relationship

Most relationships are sustainable as long as at least one party makes a need-to-have level of effort. Unless, of course, they expect equal reciprocity, become resentful, and stop trying.

SHORT LIST, LONG GAME

A large part of the work that goes into maintaining a Short List is managing your feelings of rejection. There may be extended periods of time when the people on your list are unresponsive. Your clients only need you when they have a problem that requires your services. Otherwise, they may go dark. Your connectors will only view you as a need-to-have if you make connections for them, as they do for you. Unless your prospects have an immediate need for your offerings, they may put off their response until later. In such moments, it's essential to remember that to maintain your Short List you must play the long game. Don't take their lack of effort personally. Don't give up. Be persistent. For most of these relationships, you stand to gain more than they do, so continue to make the effort, even absent theirs. That way, they can respond and reconnect when it's convenient for them.

This imbalanced dynamic explains why your Short List needs to be manageable in scope. When doing the heavy lifting, you can only maintain a small number of need-to-have relationships because they require a significant amount of effort. But consider that your attention is one of the ways you show your appreciation for the important impact they either currently have or will have in your life.

Reminding People that they Matter

I spent some time with author, professor, and psychologist Doğan Cüceloğlu many years ago. During our conversation, he shared his thoughts on the basic human need for social validation. He explained that people need to feel like they matter, and one of the fundamental ways they receive that message is through respectful words, actions, and positive attention from the people around them. When you maintain contact with someone on your Short List, treating them as a need-to-have, or reconnecting with them after a period of absence, you reinforce the notion that they matter to you.

Another way to do this is to give them a genuine compliment. Studies show that a heartfelt, supportive compliment activates the same part of the brain as a monetary reward.[10] It also fulfills our basic human need for social acceptance. Your compliment may focus on one of the personal or professional accomplishments the person has shared with you or simply their responsiveness in getting back to you. As long as it is an authentic expression of your appreciation, it validates them.

Depending on your upbringing and cultural background, you

---

10 Keise Izuma, Daisuke N. Saito, and Nrihiro Sadato, "Processing of Social and Monetary Rewards in the Human Striatum," *Neuron*, 58(2), April 24, 2008, 284–294, https://www.sciencedirect.com/science/article/pii/S0896627308002663.

may have a hard time giving compliments. You may worry about how others will perceive your words, so you mostly keep your praise to yourself. You are not alone—most people receive very little guidance on how to compliment effectively. So here are a few tips to help you acknowledge the people who matter to you.

- **Don't get hung up on the words.** I spoke to Dr. Xuan Zhao about the study she and Nicholas Epley conducted on compliments when she was at Stanford. She confirmed that most people underestimate the impact a simple compliment can have. They may overthink how they should say it, and often end up saying nothing. For the compliment receiver, the phraseology comes second. It's the warmth behind it that has the impact.[11]

- **Be specific.** Generic statements like, "you're awesome" and "great job" are far less meaningful than compliments that call out the discrete things that impressed you.

- **Avoid complimenting their physical appearance.** Some people are self-conscious about the way they look or may become uncomfortable by a comment that could be construed as flirtatious or inappropriate.

- **Use the ACT method.** ACT stands for the three areas where you should focus your compliments:

  - Accomplishments: Their specific achievements or successes.

  - Competencies: Their skills, talents, or expertise.

---

11 Xuan Zhao and Nicholas Epley, "Insufficiently Complimentary? Underestimating the Positive Impact of Compliments Creates a Barrier to Expressing Them," *Journal of Personality and Social Psychology*, 121(2), 2021, 239–256, https://doi.org/10.1037/pspa0000277.

- Traits: Their positive non-physical characteristics, such as kindness, determination, or creativity.

By following these guidelines, you can make your compliments more impactful and meaningful, reinforcing your connections and making the people on your Short List feel truly valued.

One of the ways I like to practice this skill in a socially safe, low-stakes environment is by complimenting the most influential people in my neighborhood. When I dine at a restaurant, my objective is to form a relationship with the most senior person in that establishment. I ask to speak with the manager, or owner if they are present. When I meet them, I compliment them on the food, the staff, the ambiance, or whatever else I enjoyed about the experience they helped to create. I also make a note of their name in my phone so I can ask for them personally the next time I visit their establishment.

The following exercise will help you practice the art of giving compliments in the same vein. Notice how applying it to the people in your Short List helps you sustain and even deepen those connections.

Exercise: Practicing Effective Compliments in Low-Stakes Environments

 10–20 minutes

This exercise will help you build confidence in giving genuine compliments and prepare you to use this technique with the people on your Short List. Follow these steps to practice and refine your complimenting skills:

Step 1: Choose Your Locations

Identify a few places you frequently visit, such as:

- Restaurants

- Barbershops or salons

- Local stores

Step 2: Engage with Management

When you visit these places, ask to speak with the manager or owner. Your objective is to form a relationship with the most senior person in that establishment.

Step 3: Deliver Specific Compliments

Compliment them on something specific about their establishment. Use one of the following types of compliments:

- Accomplishments: "I really appreciate everyone's professionalism here. You've clearly put a lot of effort into hiring and training your team."

- Competencies: "The food here is always delicious. You are an amazing chef."

- Traits: "Your attention to detail is exceptional. I'm really impressed by your work."

Step 4: Note Their Name

After meeting them, make a note of their name in your phone so you can ask for them personally the next time you visit.

Step 5: Repeat and Reflect

The next time you visit their establishment, ask for them by name. If you feel inclined, compliment them on something new. If not, just spend a few moments checking in with them, so they know that they matter enough to warrant your time and attention. Notice how learning their name and giving even one specific compliment elevates your relationship with them and your experience of visiting their establishment. Pay attention to how these interactions make you feel more confident in delivering compliments.

Step 6: Apply to Your Short List

Once you've practiced this technique in low-stakes environments, start using it more often with the people on your Short List. Compliment their accomplishments, competencies, and non-physical traits. Notice how it helps you sustain and even deepen those connections.

Scan this QR code to download a PDF of this exercise and the corresponding worksheets.

Chapter 11

Targeting

The idea behind targeting may seem counterintuitive given the approach you've taken so far to build your Short List. But in addition to the people you already know, and the people you've met by networking in accessible communities, you need 10 to 20 percent of your Short List to consist of perfect strangers who fit the profile of your high-value client. Your objective will be to get to know them and, over time, develop a relationship that leads to your first engagement with them.

This exercise is important because, no matter how well-connected you may be, there are prospects beyond your immediate reach whose business can make all the difference in your success. In fact, without them, you can spend years running in place, focused on the same low- and medium-value opportunities that currently make up your book of business. But when you get proactive about identifying high-value targets, thoughtful about connecting with them, and intentional about helping them, you position yourself for consideration when they have the right project for your expertise. None of that is possible if they've never heard of you.

CLIENT PROFILE ANALYSIS

This chapter will walk you through the process of profiling your typical current client and comparing them to the profile of a high-value client. At the end of the chapter, you can use the Client Profiler Worksheet to apply your insights and analyze your results.

First, consider the typical client you currently serve so you can see how close or far you are from a high-value book of business. Reflect on the profile that currently makes up the lion's share of your clientele, starting with your typical client's demographics.

- Age: What is the age range of your typical client?

- Geography: Are they based in a specific geographical area?

- Culture: While cultural background may not be a relevant demographic, notice whether your cultural characteristics attract clients who share the same background.

- Industry: Is there a common industry or niche focus among your current clients?

Next, identify your typical current client's psychographics. These are the thoughts and feelings that drive their decisions.

- Key objectives: Are your current clients mostly focused on topline growth, profitability, minimizing liabilities, cornering their market, or is there another objective that tends to drive their business behavior?

- Chief concerns: What keeps your current clients up at night? Are they in a highly competitive or price-sensitive marketplace?

The third category in your Client Profiler will focus on the service needs in your current client base.

- Offerings: What specific offerings do your clients engage you for the most?

- Level of expertise: Do your clients currently come to you for work you must do yourself, or can you delegate a good portion of it to more junior people on your team? If it's the former, you will not be able to scale or leverage.

- Frequency of need: How often do your current clients come to you for help, on average. Once a year? Quarterly? Or do you maintain clients who reach out to you with a new need every month?

- Trigger circumstances: What are the circumstances that trigger the demand for your services? A letter from the IRS? A cyber breach? An unexpected termination?

- Decision-makers: What is the typical title of the highest influence-scorer who engages your services? Do you mostly deal with the VP of Sales? Head of Finance? Someone else?

Finally, consider your clients' personal interests. Are they football fans? Wine drinkers? Hikers? Are many of them parents of small children? The more their interests match your own, the more opportunities you will have for social time. If you aren't sure about their personal interests, consider that you haven't made enough of an effort to form a relationship with them.

Now, consider your high-value client profile and think through the same process. Imagine your book of business was made up of ideal clients. What would the typical demographics be in terms of age, geography, culture, and industry? Then move to psychographics, including key objectives and chief concerns. Again, these psychographics reflect the ideal level of sophistication and profitability aligned with your vision of a high-value client. Next, what do you anticipate in terms of their service needs? Bigger projects will necessitate more leverage and higher fees. What is a reasonable expectation for their frequency of need? What circumstances do clients at this level encounter that trigger a need for your services? Is the decision-maker the VP of Sales or will they need the CEO's approval at this higher level of outsourcing? Finally, consider their personal interests. What kinds of leisure activities are your high-value clients likely to make time for?

As you'll recall from the earlier chapter on influence scoring, people tend to gravitate toward others who are just like them. You may see this reflected when you review the profile of your typical current client, as it's likely that many of their characteristics resemble your own. So, if your demographics don't fit the profile of your high-value client, it's because you're involved in activities that are exposing you to low-value and medium-value prospects.

EXAMPLES OF CLIENT PROFILE ANALYSIS

Let's consider Jamie, a junior partner at a law firm. When she profiles her high-value clients, she describes in-house litigation and HR leaders. But when she considers her social circle, it consists mostly of coworkers at her firm, fellow board members at a local charity clinic where she volunteers, and her local friends and family. The referrals she's received from these avenues have turned out to be low-value prospects with local startups. Jamie will have a hard time achieving her ambitious SMART goals if she doesn't gain access to communities with higher demographics, psychographics, and service needs.

Then, there's Mark, a management consultant. His ideal clients are the C-Suite of middle-market and emerging growth companies. But when he looks at his existing network, it's mostly made up of colleagues from his consulting firm, the contacts he's made in the professional services space, and an assortment of foodies who've found their way into his wine club. One or two of them fit the high-value client profile, but most of them are just like him, with moderate practices and business needs. His business will continue to plateau unless he starts surrounding himself with more profitable demographics, psychographics, and service needs.

Both Mark and Jamie have the same challenge: If they focus exclusively on their current networks and activities, they will be bogged down by low-value and medium-value opportunities. It will take years for their existing networks to mature into high-value clients, and without a proactive plan, their business development will continue to flounder.

When Jamie looks at the Client Profiler, she sees that her ideal client is typically a female business leader holding a senior role within a middle-market organization. She participates in at least one trade association and often attends professional development seminars and conferences. But she is inundated by invitations to generic functions and presentations. When viewed through the lens of Jamie's existing conditions, these characteristics can be discouraging.

But if Jamie recalibrates her approach to align with her high-value client profile, new opportunities emerge. Jamie joins SHRM

(Society for Human Resources Management), a well-known international trade association, which gives her access to HR leaders at a variety of organizations. She contacts the local programming committee at SHRM with an offer to moderate an upcoming panel at their next local event. She asks two women GCs who are high-value clients at her firm to be panelists. During their prep meeting, they share a few insights that inspire Jamie to create a new seminar on labor and employment trends. She markets her seminar to her firm contacts, and to various other HR-focused trade associations. Finally, she invites her panelists to participate in a women's business leaders' roundtable in conjunction with a women's initiative at her firm. Within a year, Jamie's activities, network, and engagements are in line with the high-value client work she has always wanted to attract.

JAMIE'S CLIENT PROFILER WORKSHEET		
	TYPICAL CURRENT CLIENT	**HIGH-VALUE CLIENT**
DEMOGRAPHICS		
Age	30–40	40–55
Geography	Chicago area	USA/International
Culture	Any	Female executive
Industry	Startups	In-house HR or litigation lead at middle-market company or larger
PSYCHOGRAPHICS		
Key Objectives	Reduce costs	Reduce risk
Chief Outcomes	Feeling like they have an advisor on-call	Experienced counsel that makes them look good to their board and stays on budget
SERVICE NEEDS		
Offerings	Mostly employee handbooks and occasional HR advice	Sophisticated litigation counsel

Level of Expertise	Low	High
Frequency of Need	Monthly	2x/year
Trigger Circumstances	Any HR challenge	Any HR challenge, some M&A
Decision-Makers	Founder	GC, Head of HR, Head of litigation
PERSONAL INTERESTS		
Interest 1	Family activities—small children	Couple's activities
Interest 2	Yoga	Travel

Mark's high-value prospect holds the C title at a company and tends to have a well-established professional network. In the past, Mark has interpreted this to mean that there will be limited interest in meeting yet another service provider, but when he views this challenge through the lens of his Client Profiler, he sees the opportunity to change his approach. First, he carves out a dedicated block in his busy schedule for a more consistent focus on business development. He scales back his participation in internal firm committees and delegates his low-value and medium-value clients to junior colleagues. This frees up time for thought leadership and networking, both of which Mark enjoys but never seems to get around to. Within a few months, he authors and publishes two new articles that showcase his expertise in penetrating new markets through strategic acquisitions. Next, he schedules meetings with each of the connectors in his Short List. His agenda for these meetings is threefold:

1. Find out what they are working on and help wherever possible.

2. Share his target profile and request introductions.

3. Share his recent articles, so his connectors can provide an example of Mark's expertise when they make the introduction.

This systematic approach exposes Mark to more high-value client opportunities. Soon after that, his book of business upgrades accordingly.

MARK'S CLIENT PROFILER WORKSHEET		
	TYPICAL CURRENT CLIENT	**HIGH-VALUE CLIENT**
DEMOGRAPHICS		
Age	30–50	40–65
Geography	San Diego	California
Culture	Any	Any
Industry	Professional services	Emerging growth industries
PSYCHOGRAPHICS		
Key Objectives	Define strategy	Refine strategy, especially for new go-to-market opportunities
Chief Outcomes	Less conflict	More growth
SERVICE NEEDS		
Offerings	Strategic planning	Strategic planning and execution
Level of Expertise	Low	High
Frequency of Need	2- to 4-month engagements. Rarely re-engage.	6- to 12-month engagements. Re-engage every 2 to 3 years.
Trigger Circumstances	Partner disagreements. Succession issues.	Acquisitions. Opportunities to enter new markets.
Decision-Makers	MP/MD/CFO/COO	CEO, CSO, Board of directors
PERSONAL INTERESTS		
Interest 1	Watching sports at a bar	Attending sports event at the stadium
Interest 2	Wine and travel	Fine wine and luxury travel

Navigating the Transition

At first, this transition may be a struggle. You will have to adjust the activities that fill your time and the company you keep until you surround yourself with high-value prospects. Most people are reluctant to make the sacrifices necessary to shift out of their existing paradigm, even if it serves their ultimate objectives. But if you're willing to take the necessary steps, you will expand into new communities and grow your book of business in short order.

Here's an example of how this played out with one of our consulting firm clients: Before they started targeting, they maintained a book of business of approximately a hundred clients each year, made up of mostly midsized companies, with a few outliers on either end of the marketplace. When they segmented their clients into low-, medium-, and high-value revenue categories, they discovered that seventy of them were low-value, twenty-five were medium-value, and only five were in the high-value category. Those five alone represented over 35 percent of their total revenue.

Every year, they would work hard to exceed the expectations of their one hundred clients. In most years, they would see somewhere between 5-to-10 percent year-over-year organic growth. Some of their low- and medium-value clients would move on, some expanded their scope, and their business development efforts would bring in a few new accounts every year. But once they started targeting high-value clients with the specific objective of bringing on five more just like the ones they had, they increased their revenue by another 30 percent. Add that to their predictable organic growth and the upshot was a 35 percent increase in their topline revenue. This is why targeting is so important if your objective is to scale your business to new heights.

Exercise: Complete the Client Profiler

 5–10 minutes

Use the left column to describe your typical current client and the right column to profile your ideal high-value client. Consider these characteristics as you seek out new prospects for your Short List.

THE CLIENT PROFILER WORKSHEET		
	TYPICAL CURRENT CLIENT	**HIGH-VALUE CLIENT**
DEMOGRAPHICS		
Age		
Geography		
Culture		
Industry		
PSYCHOGRAPHICS		
Key Objectives		
Chief Outcomes		
SERVICE NEEDS		
Offerings		
Level of Expertise		
Frequency of Need		
Trigger Circumstances		
Decision-Makers		
PERSONAL INTERESTS		
Interest 1		
Interest 2		

Scan this QR code to download a PDF of this exercise and the corresponding worksheets.

Chapter 12

Successful Engagement Strategies

Participants often come to our business development training and coaching programs with unrealistic expectations. They are smart, busy people who have worked hard to develop expertise in their field. They have a sense of professional pride and healthy egos. They want their expertise to sell itself. This puts them into a mostly passive stance, waiting for someone to be impressed by their bio or thought leadership and reach out with a request for help. That's why so much of their business is reliant on referrals. A referral from a trusted source introduces the prospect into the middle of the buying process, grappling with an immediate problem and open to hearing a pitch from the right solution.

That same provider will work hard to meet client expectations on an initial project, hoping their hard work will speak for itself, and eventually, expand the scope of work. But without regular prompting and education, most clients repeatedly call with the same need rather than cross-sell themselves into the various other ways their providers can help.

If you're happy with your current book of business, a passive stance is fine. Keep doing what you're doing, hang out, and wait for the next opportunity; it's clearly working. But if you are committed to expanding your book of business, you must proactively target high-value prospects and convert their journey through the seven buying stages. And because you view them as need-to-haves, while they mainly consider you a nice-to-have in their network, you must take the lead on outreach.

Unfortunately, most business development occurs in our imagination. We have a meeting with a prospect. We feel the meeting went well. We imagine they are going to engage. But they often don't. We have a great conversation with a client. The client implies they will call us when they are ready to engage additional work. We imagine they are just waiting for the right time, only to learn a year later that they hired a competitor.

To improve your effectiveness in business development, you'll need to get out of your head and into the game. Measure your progress using an empirical model based not on subjective assumptions of where you think you stand with your prospect but based solely on their actions. Actions speak louder than words. Observe what your prospect is doing, not what you think they will do. Their actions tell you beyond a shadow of a doubt where you are in the engagement process and what you need to advance it to the next stage.

THE SEVEN STAGES OF ENGAGEMENT

There are seven engagement stages when converting a B2B prospect into a loyal client: acknowledge, follow, respond, meet, pitch, engage, and expand. If you're the type of person who likes a good acronym, I'm afraid all we have here is AFRMPEE.

Acknowledge

You've added a target to your Short List with the intention of converting them into a high-value client. You have no relationship with them. They don't know you exist. Your objective is to share relevant thought leadership that compels your busy prospect to acknowledge it. This probably won't happen on your first try. It will likely take several attempts before they click on one of your links, read your posts, or visit your website, but any of these actions will indicate that you piqued their interest in something that warrants their time and attention.

You may have heard of the "rule of seven," which is a commonly held marketing principle stating that it takes seven "touches" to familiarize someone with your brand. Apparently, the concept was coined in the 1930s by Hollywood movie studios, who discovered they had to expose movie-goers to the movie poster of any given film an average of seven times before they would consider buying a ticket.

To get a target from the initial stage of "acknowledge" to the second stage "follow," start with the "seven touches" principle, sharing relevant information, invitations, and personalized communications, but keep in mind that you are not a 1930s movie mogul. Your prospect may acknowledge you the very first time they encounter your information, they may do so after seven touches, or only after several dozen.

For example, you found Sharon Murphy on LinkedIn. She's the general counsel at a pharmaceutical company who fits your high-value client profile. You sent her a personalized email, introducing yourself, referencing a few connections you share on LinkedIn, and enclosing a link to an article you wrote about the latest litigation trends in pharma. You mentioned that you'd be happy to chat with her about her reaction to the article. She did not respond, but your outbound marketing stats show that she clicked the link to your article. It may not feel like much, but this is significant progress. By acknowledging interest in your thought leadership, your target signaled a potential need for your services. The process of building a relationship around that need can begin.

Follow

When your prospect starts to follow your output repeatedly, it means that they consider you to be a credible source of information worth incorporating into their professional knowledge feed. This indicates a growing level of interest in the value you can provide.

To advance a prospect from a one-off acknowledgment to the state of following you, you'll need to consistently deliver high-quality, relevant content that aligns with their interests and challenges. By regularly sharing thought leadership that showcases your expertise and demonstrates your deep understanding of their industry, you build momentum on their initial interest and increase the likelihood that they will participate in a dialogue.

To continue our example, once Sharon acknowledged your initial outreach, you sent her another article and a personalized connection request, which she accepted. As soon as you saw the LinkedIn notification, you sent her a direct message on LinkedIn thanking her for connecting with you and letting her know of an upcoming webinar that might be of interest. Her response was a simple, "Nice to meet you" with no reference to the webinar. While her response may have been brief, she took the time to write back, indicating her receptivity to further engagement efforts.

Respond

Your target replied to your outreach. You have shared at least one back-and-forth communication. Your continuous outreach communicates your genuine interest in speaking with your prospect. Once you get to the respond stage, anticipate several outreach attempts before they are willing to meet. To incentivize a meeting, propose an agenda you can cover in fifteen to twenty minutes that serves their interests and aligns with their needs. Make sure they understand this is not a pitch.

Back to Sharon, you clicked the bell icon on her LinkedIn profile so you'd be notified of all her posts. Before long, she announced that her department was making a hire. You sent a direct message that you would keep an eye out for relevant candidates from your network. You also continued to send her thought leadership and invitations to webinars, which occasionally garnered polite responses. Then Sharon attended one of your webinars and indicated on your poll that she'd be open to a follow-up conversation. You sent her an email, asking what she would like to discuss, replied with a proposed agenda based on her request, and scheduled a meeting for the following week. Things are moving in the right direction.

Meet

Your prospect is willing to spend a few minutes with you, typically for a complimentary, exploratory consultation. Don't monopolize the meeting with a monologue about your background, trying to impress them with your extensive knowledge. Come to the meeting prepared with questions that help you understand their situation so that your comments are attuned to their needs. Offer a relevant value-add with tangible value, such as a helpful resource ("here is a

checklist that can improve your internal process"), free work product ("we would be willing to update your employee handbook so
it includes the latest overtime regulations free of charge"), or an
insightful piece of information ("we wanted to make you aware of
an interesting trend among the clients we serve in your industry").
Leading with value makes a positive first impression and increases
the likelihood that they will meet with you again.

This can be the most time-consuming stage. In B2B professional
services, where the product is the provider, it will take numerous interactions as you get to know them, get to know their business, they get
to know you, and you connect the dots between their needs and your
solution. Once you have earned their trust and are top of mind when
the need for your expertise arises, you will be invited to pitch.

In your meeting with Sharon, you asked smart questions and,
only then, explained how you could help. She was impressed with the
value-adds you offered. She shared that she's looking to make a change
in litigation counsel and asked follow-up questions about your trial
experience. She seemed satisfied with your responses and said she'd
keep you in mind for an upcoming Request for Proposal (RFP).

Pitch

They have a time-sensitive need for your solution and want to have
a conversation about the possibility of hiring you. They will likely be
considering multiple options, including a few of your competitors or
insourcing the need if they can. So, your solution needs to address
their pain point in a compelling manner. Note that because you are
an untested provider, a one-off, small project or pilot is more likely
to be awarded than a large one.

The complexity of the pitch stage depends on multiple factors, but in most B2B contexts, it includes a competitive bid of some sort. There could be an RFQ (request for qualifications), RFP (request for proposal), proposal, influencer pitch meeting, decision-maker pitch meeting, negotiations with the procurement department, the satisfaction of technical requirements related to competencies, or compliance with IT/security protocols. The more involved your offering, and the more regulated your industry, the more steps this stage will have.

Continuing our journey with Sharon, you thought after the exploratory meeting that she would follow up with an RFP, but she went dark. She stopped clicking your links or attending your webinars. You started worrying that you might have said the wrong thing in your meeting with her, or that she'd simply moved on. Months later she resurfaced, letting you know that her department continues to be understaffed and that she needs to engage litigation counsel right away. She asked that you submit a proposal and prepare a formal pitch for Sharon and a few of her colleagues from the litigation department. The pitch went well, and they said they would let you know their decision soon. In the meantime, you connected with their team on LinkedIn, sent them the follow-up materials you promised, and invited them to an upcoming seminar you're presenting on a relevant topic.

Engage

Congratulations, you're hired! The pitch was a success, and an engagement is in effect. This is a critical opportunity to establish a strong first impression, validate the client's decision to work with your firm, and set the tone for a productive and successful collaboration. There are several best practices to adopt into your kickoff to ensure a positive start.

First, get to know the client's team. Building relationships with key stakeholders lays the foundation for a successful long-term partnership. During the onboarding meeting, make note of their roles, responsibilities, and any unique details that might inform personalized communications in the future. Delve into their objectives and expectations for the project, including key milestones, timelines, and any potential challenges they anticipate. Ask about their communication preferences. Are they partial to informal check-ins, weekly formal status updates, or something in between? Would they rather receive emails or discuss in real time? Is it okay to send a text on the weekend if a time-sensitive issue arises? And who should you try to reach if your main point of contact is offline or unavailable? Clarifying these details upfront fosters smooth communication and ensures everyone is on the same page.

Sharon's team certainly appreciated the thorough list of questions you brought to your onboarding session. It helped them think through their specific objectives and preferences. At the end of the meeting, Sharon said, "Well, team, we're clearly in good hands." Her colleagues agreed, and the tenor in their conference room was palpably optimistic.

Expand

The client completed their initial work with you. You have every reason to believe they will come back to you with a similar need, but cross-selling is another matter. You'll need to expand the relationship to turn them into a high-value client. The good news is that this stage is typically much easier than the stages that preceded it as long as you understand the specifics around your client's business well enough to anticipate the additional services they may require. You've already earned their trust for the first piece of work. Now, you must position yourself to earn more significant projects.

Many providers get to the expand stage and assume the work they're getting is the extent of the work available. After all, your clients know all your firm's capabilities, don't they? And they certainly know where to find you should a need arise. But these assumptions rarely prove to be accurate.

As you're servicing the work, look for ways to foster deeper relationships with the client's team. Ask questions during the engagement that help you understand their business holistically so you can identify needs that warrant expansive solutions. And add unexpected value beyond the scope of engaged work.

After a successful outcome on your first case for Sharon, she assures you there will be more work soon. But months pass with no word, so you get proactive. You propose a site visit to get to know the team better, present an in-person education program, and perform an onsite liability audit. At first, they don't seem interested in your offer. So, you continue to send thought leadership, and you ask their Head of Litigation to contribute a few thoughts to an article you're authoring. The interview affords the opportunity to ask questions about his specific challenges and the pharma company's goals. He seems to appreciate your perspective, and shortly thereafter, you receive an invitation to visit their main office to present your program and perform your audit.

Your site visit was instrumental in developing relationships with the various people on Sharon's team. You now have a better sense of the additional areas where they need help (mostly corporate and data privacy), you know the kind of education they need, and you've learned that you and Sharon share a passion for '90s grunge bands. Your emails to her are more personalized (asking about her kids and occasionally referencing your favorite Pearl Jam album). Your invitations to webinars presented by your data privacy and M&A partners are well-received. Within six months, Sharon's team has engaged two additional lines of service at the firm, and because of the strong relationship you've developed with her, Sharon consults you first whenever she has litigation concerns. In less than two years, her pharma company went from being a target on your Short List to one of your largest clients.

THE SEVEN STAGES OF ENGAGEMENT

Based on the actions a prospect, connector, or client take in their engagement journey.

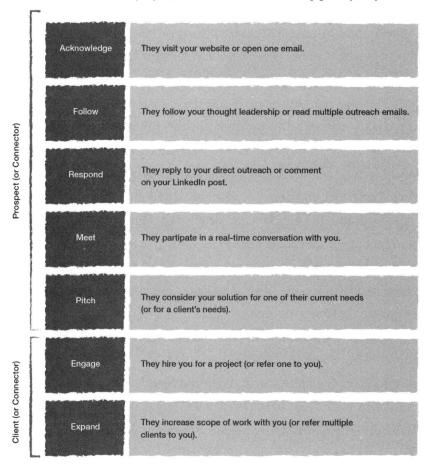

Acknowledge	They visit your website or open one email.
Follow	They follow your thought leadership or read multiple outreach emails.
Respond	They reply to your direct outreach or comment on your LinkedIn post.
Meet	They partipate in a real-time conversation with you.
Pitch	They consider your solution for one of their current needs (or for a client's needs).
Engage	They hire you for a project (or refer one to you).
Expand	They increase scope of work with you (or refer multiple clients to you).

Prospect (or Connector) — Acknowledge, Follow, Respond, Meet, Pitch

Client (or Connector) — Engage, Expand

In our business development training and coaching programs, we are often asked about the total number of interactions required to advance a contact through all seven stages of engagement. The answer depends on numerous factors including whether the contact in question is a prospect, client, or connector; the number of unique commonalities you share; whether they like you personally; which industry you hail from; the complexity of your offering; the stage of your career; and the skill with which you apply many of the concepts in this book. Given that connectors make it their business to meet new people and add value, you may find that you accelerate quickly to the engage stage, where they give you information, introductions, or referrals, and advance to the expand stage with even more value soon after that. Prospects who come through a successful RFP process or referral tend to close quickly. Targeted prospects with no prior history of engagement with your firm take much longer. Based on our PipelinePlus Tracker user data, and various informal surveys conducted among buyers over the years, we have found that very few engage B2B professional services with an unknown firm inside of fourteen interactions.

Given that most pursuers give up after only one or two unsuccessful follow-ups (if they follow up at all), any business developer with the patience and persistence to take at least fourteen proactive actions has a considerable advantage. While it's good to track your pursuit data to determine your average, recognize that the higher-value pursuits will often take longer. In the meantime, focus on the one thing that is within your control: your next proactive action.

FORTY ACTIONS THAT ADVANCE CONTACTS THROUGH THE SEVEN STAGES OF ENGAGEMENT

We just reviewed several outreach tactics that advanced Sharon through the seven engagement stages. The following is a list of forty proactive actions you can take to accelerate your momentum with each of the people on your Short List. The following matrix will show you which of these actions are more appropriate for contacts you've just started targeting, versus the actions better suited to people you've already met, or client relationships you're looking to expand. Depending on how aggressive or conservative you tend to be in your approach, you may choose to take some of these actions at earlier or later engagement stages. At any given time, choose the action that makes the most sense given your comfort level, your relationship with the person, where they are in the engagement process, and whether they are primarily a prospect, client, or connector.

It's important to note that these actions collectively build positive, long-term relationships. They stand in contrast to the short-sighted, transactional mindset many professionals have, pitching their services too early and giving up if there's no immediate benefit. The focus here is not on what you can sell, but how you can help. This approach is especially crucial when dealing with your Short List—the most valuable people in your network. Given their high influence scores, they likely encounter superficial pitches all the time. The key is to defer your self-interest and nurture your relationships over time. Expect to contribute value multiple times before you receive anything in return. This way, you capture their interest in the short term and earn their loyalty in the long run. The net result over time builds a network of deal givers, which is considerably more profitable than chasing after the next deal.

FORTY ACTIONS MATRIX

	ACTION	ENGAGEMENT STAGE						
		Acknowledge	Follow	Respond	Meet	Pitch	Engage	Expand
1	Research their background and current situation	X	X	X	X	X	X	X
2	Connect on social media	X	X	X	X	X	X	X
3	Look up their latest posts on LinkedIn and comment	X	X	X	X	X	X	X
4	Consume their thought leadership (writings, panels, podcast interviews) and send a complimentary note with your reaction	X	X	X	X	X	X	X
5	Point out commonalities (shared contacts, shared backgrounds, hobbies, interests)	X	X	X	X	X	X	X
6	Send them insights from industry thought leaders (articles, studies, videos, books, etc.)	X	X	X	X	X	X	X
7	Send personalized invitations to your webinars and seminars	X	X	X	X	X	X	X
8	Post professional content on LinkedIn and respond to comments	X	X	X	X	X	X	X
9	Share appropriate personal interests on LinkedIn and respond to comments	X	X	X	X	X	X	X
10	Create and send helpful business resources (checklists, industry studies, trends)	X	X	X	X	X	X	X
11	Interview them as contributors to your written thought leadership (blogs or articles)	X	X	X	X	X	X	X
12	Invite them to local, firm-hosted social events	X	X	X	X	X	X	X

		Acknowledge	Follow	Respond	Meet	Pitch	Engage	Expand
13	Invite them to be a panelist or copresenter at a webinar or live program			X	X	X	X	X
14	Send them a note or card on special occasions (birthdays, holidays)			X	X	X	X	X
15	Ask for their perspective			X	X	X	X	X
16	Offer a second opinion			X	X	X	X	X
17	Propose an exploratory strategy session, where you advise on their current challenges and emerging issues				X	X	X	X
18	Pay them a genuine compliment (focus on achievements, competencies, and inherent traits)				X	X	X	X
19	Recommend a good restaurant, hotel, or activity in their area				X	X	X	X
20	Introduce them to a relevant connector				X	X	X	X
21	Monitor job postings and facilitate new hires				X	X	X	X
22	Invite them to join you at an industry conference or seminar				X	X	X	X
23	Whenever local, arrange face time over a drink or meal				X	X	X	X
24	Invite them to a unique experience (sporting event, concert)				X	X	X	X
25	Send a follow-up note, thanking them for their time, advice, or anything else they did that was helpful to you				X	X	X	X
26	Update them on your latest capabilities and introduce them to new team members				X	X	X	X

		Acknowledge	Follow	Respond	Meet	Pitch	Engage	Expand
27	Ask about their long-term business goals and challenges				X	X	X	X
28	Check in informally to see how they're doing						X	X
29	Write a LinkedIn recommendation for them						X	X
30	Request a LinkedIn recommendation from them						X	X
31	Request an introduction to a high-value prosect or connector						X	X
32	Highlight them in your newsletter or on social media						X	X
33	Conduct a case study or joint press release on your work together						X	X
34	Give a gift or a GET						X	X
35	Conduct a client feedback interview						X	X
36	Conduct a needs assessment						X	X
37	Propose a bespoke educational webinar or seminar just for their team						X	X
38	Propose a client site visit at their offices						X	X
39	Offer complimentary training or mentoring for junior members of their team						X	X
40	Review the charities and causes in their social media and on their website. Contribute to the ones that align with your values.						X	X

A detailed description of each action, with specific examples, is available on our website.

Scan this QR code to download a PDF of this exercise and the corresponding worksheets.

Actions 1–12 are generally appropriate at the earliest stages of targeting, and throughout the engagement process.

Actions 13–16 are best timed once the contact has responded to your outreach, indicating their interest in a two-way exchange.

Actions 17–27 are best suited to contacts at the meet stage, with whom you are actively developing a relationship and vetting them for long-term consideration on your Short List.

Actions 28–40 are best suited to clients at the engage and expand stages, or prospects and connectors with whom you've developed strong relationships.

To use this list effectively, scan the forty actions, concentrating on the ones that align to your contact's position in the engagement process. For early-stage targets, use the first group of actions. The more you advance through the engagement process with someone, the more actions become available to you. For example, it's always a good idea to research their background (action #1), as you will likely learn something new, even if the contact in question is a long-standing client. But it is neither appropriate nor effective to ask an early-stage target you haven't yet met about the charities and causes they support so you can make a donation (action #40). That action only resonates with someone you've moved through the stages of acknowledge, respond, meet, and pitch. Otherwise, the gesture feels manipulative and presumptuous. The early-stage actions grant access to the later-stage actions.

Also, I encourage you to be selective about the actions you use. Some of them simply won't resonate for you. Others will work well in combination and may become your go-to. If you arrange face time over a drink or meal (action #23), you can also check in informally (#28), ask about their business goals and challenges (#27), and send a thank you note afterwards (#25). If you ever feel stuck, wondering what you can do to proactively move a relationship to the next stage of engagement, the Forty Actions Matrix will be a helpful reference.

WHAT IT TAKES TO STAY TOP OF MIND

According to a Thomson Reuters survey of more than four hundred B2B buyers, maintaining recent contact is the most effective way to generate new business opportunities.[12] Unlike factors such as specialization, location, or reputation, which had a modest 13 to 23 percent impact on engagement likelihood, staying top of mind through recent contact drove 70 percent of buying decisions. This means that if you consistently connect with your prospects and

---

12   Thomson Reuters, "Global Elite Law Firm Brand Index 2022," 2022, https://www.thomsonreuters.com/en-us/posts/wp-content/uploads/sites/20/2022/01/Global-Elite-Law-Firm-Brand-Index-2022_FINAL.pdf.

clients, you're significantly more likely to be the first choice when they're ready to outsource a project.

Consider this your secret weapon in the competitive landscape. Even if your rivals have larger marketing budgets, deeper industry expertise, or stronger reputations, staying in regular touch with your prospects can give you a decisive advantage. To achieve this, aim for monthly outreach. Our survey of over one thousand professionals across various industries in the same year found that reaching out every four to six weeks is considered optimal. Anything more was thought to be too aggressive.

If you're in the pitch phase with a prospect, tailor your follow-ups to align with their requests and timeline. They may ask for a proposal by a certain date, or references within a given timeframe, but if you're looking simply to stay top of mind, aim to take a proactive action every four weeks. This consistent, yet considerate, approach will help you build lasting connections and increase your chances of securing valuable opportunities.

Exercise: Find Your Favored Actions

 2–5 minutes

Step 1: Identify Preferred Actions
Review the Forty Actions Matrix and use a highlighter to indicate the actions you find most comfortable given your personality, brand, and the unique prospect expectations in your industry.

Step 2: Apply Preferred Actions

Reference your list of preferred actions when advancing a target through the seven stages of engagement.

Scan this QR code to download a PDF of this exercise and the corresponding worksheets.

Chapter 13

Adding Value in Every Interaction

Let's take a moment to talk about proactive actions that *don't* work. Click on your spam folder and review the email messages you've ignored over the past few days. Better yet, let me save you some time and tell you what's waiting for you there.

1. An attempt to grab your attention by using your first name in the subject line but generic messaging in the body of the message. You've never heard of the sender.

2. A message that launches right into a pitch, suggesting that you're missing out on either revenue or savings unless you act now.

3. A message that tries to make you feel guilty for not responding to the sender's last email. Or the five that preceded it in their automated cadence.

4. An email from a persistent company whose mail list you could've sworn you unsubscribed from a few months back.

What do these senders have in common? They made no effort to build a relationship or earn your trust before making their pitch. Their spray and pray strategy relies on high-volume outreach and the hope that some very small percentage of their email list will respond with interest in their product or service. This approach often leads to reputation damage with the majority of their recipients, who were inconvenienced and annoyed by the spam. Contrast this to personalization, a more respectful strategy that requires more time upfront and a smaller target list but has a much higher rate of success.

PERSONALIZE YOUR INTERACTIONS

Take a lesson from the spammers and avoid generic openers, even when you send a message to an established relationship, like someone on your Short List. Here is an example of a typical generic opener addressed to a known contact, compared to a personalized one.

Generic: Hi Barbara. I hope this finds you well.

Personalized: Hi Barbara. It's been a few months since we last connected. I hope you're keeping dry with all the rain in Boston this week. I see from your LinkedIn posts that you've had a busy summer. I'm intrigued by the talk you gave at the SAE conference last month and would be interested to hear about it when we next speak. I'll be in Boston soon and

would like to meet up. Perhaps we could have lunch
at Row 34—I've been craving those delicious lobster
rolls since my last visit . . .

In the second example, the sender makes a thoughtful effort to
delve into Barbara's world, taking the time to research her location
and the weather she is experiencing. They also reference her LinkedIn
posts and show interest in the talk she gave at a recent conference.
They mention their last visit to Boston to elevate the connection
further and reference a local restaurant Barbara may have visited.
These additional touches signify that the message was uniquely
crafted for Barbara and that she is important enough to warrant special attention.

Sales consultant Sam McKenna aptly calls this more detailed
level of personalization "Show Me You Know Me." It proves to your
contacts that they are not just a line item in a contact database but
an important individual with a unique experience that warrants
acknowledgment.

Follow this kind of personalized opening with a genuinely helpful tip or a relevant piece of information that adds value to Barbara's
day, and the message becomes a refreshing alternative to all the
other transactional emails in her inbox. The sender's willingness to
invest in a tailored message increases the likelihood that Barbara
will respond to the email, especially if she's tasted those buttery
lobster rolls.

Outreach to your Short List requires careful aim with a bow and
arrow, not peppering the landscape with a machine gun. With your
ideal client profile clearly defined, a personalized approach to communication, and a value-added action, you drastically improve your
success rate, even at the earliest stages of engagement.

FINISH STRONG

Busy professionals, flooded with various forms of communication, from emails to voicemails to texts to DMs, commonly adopt a triage mindset, focused on efficiently closing the loop and moving on to the next task. But our communications are more than just tasks to complete. Each exchange is a potential gateway to gain more information and deepen a connection. Instead of rushing to clear our inbox, let's consider how we can invite replies that enrich our relationships.

Use Closing Questions to Drive Momentum

One mistake I often see people make is to end their emails with closing statements rather than closing questions. Closing statements don't necessarily warrant a response. When you close your email message with a thoughtfully crafted question, you encourage more engagement. You also position yourself as a more proactive, responsive communicator.

For example, consider each time your firm hosts an event. Your marketing department sends an invitation to the firm's database. Many of your most important contacts receive (and often ignore) these generic invitations, which is why it's a good idea to send a personalized email to your Short List reiterating the invitation. But if your message ends with a closing statement, it will have little impact.

> "We have an event coming up, Simon. See below for details. I hope you can attend."

> "I'm forwarding the details for an upcoming event. Should be worth attending."

These statements don't require a response from Simon. They are almost as easy to ignore as the generic invitation.

But if you end your personalized note with a closing question, it lets Simon know that he not only warranted special consideration but that you genuinely want him to attend.

> "We have an event coming up, Simon. It would be great to see you there. Can you attend?"

Perhaps he can. Perhaps he can't, but either way, your closing question has a higher likelihood of prompting his response, because it communicates that Simon's attendance matters to you. Here are a few other examples contrasting closing statements with closing questions.

Closing statement:

> "Hi, Sally. I'm looking for industry events to attend in the coming months. The X-World Conference is coming up. I'd be interested to know if you've attended."

If the recipient has not attended, they may allow their non-response to be their answer. But if the message concludes with a closing question, it opens an exploration.

Closing question:

> "I'm looking for industry events to attend in the coming months. The X-World Conference is coming up. Have you attended that one?"

Closing statement:

> "I'm checking in on the proposal we sent you last month. Let me know if you have any additional

questions and when you plan to review it with your decision-makers."

If they don't have any additional questions and have yet to review the proposal with their decision-makers, this message may be deleted or flagged for future response.

Closing question:

"I'm checking in on the proposal we sent you last month. Let me know if you have any additional questions. Separately, can you tell me when you plan to review it with decision-makers?"

Incorporating a closing question into your professional email does not guarantee a response, but it invites an ongoing dialogue more effectively than the alternative. By consistently leaving the door open for responses, you cultivate an environment where communication is not just a transaction but a continuous exchange of ideas and opportunities.

BE HIGHLY RESPONSIVE

When it comes to client service, those of us in professional services aim to be highly responsive. Indeed, our clients expect it. But most professionals don't apply the same urgency to their business development. Those who do gain a strategic advantage that often separates the rainmakers from the hopefuls.

A widely cited article published by Harvard Business Review reported that many firms lose significant revenue due to slow response time. HBR surveyed over two thousand B2B professionals in sales roles across various industries, including professional services. They found that the average response time to a prospect expressing interest in their offerings was forty-two hours. This was a costly lag, considering those who responded to a prospect within an hour of receiving a query were nearly sixty times more likely to have a meaningful conversation with a key decision-maker than the average responder.[13]

The contrast is easy to imagine when you consider the scenario from your perspective. Let's say you send someone an email. They are your priority at that moment. If they respond immediately, you are more likely to engage with them than if they respond an hour or two later. By then, you will have moved on to the next thing, and their reply will sit in your inbox, along with the other accumulating items, until you find the time to sift through the backlog. That could take days or even weeks, depending on your workload.

The people on your Short List are busy, influential people, juggling professional and personal demands every day. I'm not suggesting that you should drop what you're doing every time you receive an email from one of them. As professionals, managing the influx of email is a constant challenge. But messages from your Short List should receive a different consideration than the other to-dos to be ticked off in the inbox. According to your assessment, they are the need-to-haves with the greatest potential to impact your professional goals. You help yourself every time you prioritize their communications and reciprocate the commitment of time they dedicate to you.

---

13 James B. Oldroyd, Kristina McElheran, and David Elkington, "The Short Life of Online Sales Leads," *Harvard Business Review*, March 2011, https://hbr.org/2011/03/the-short-life-of-online-sales-leads.

HOW TO NAVIGATE SMALL TALK

Similarly, we can apply the principle of personalization for more meaningful interactions when we start up a real-time conversation with them. Most superficial small talk commonly leads off with the same three general WBT questions (weather, business, travel).

Whether it's weather, business, or travel, these go-to topics require little effort on either party's part to exchange a few comments. Chances are, you've used WBT to break the ice with a new acquaintance or to avoid seeming rude at the top of a business meeting. But because WBT questions are generic in nature, they almost always result in short, boring, forgettable conversations that quickly fizzle out; they are not a useful means of vetting a Short List candidate or deepening a relationship.

Two Techniques for Better Small Talk

When your intention is to facilitate a meaningful connection, it's always better to show a genuine interest in the other person as an individual. Just as WBT prompts a general response, the *lately technique* takes the conversation to a more detailed level. For example, the question, "How is business?" will usually elicit the same handful of generic responses:

> "Fine."
> "Good."
> "The usual."
> "Really busy."

But when you follow up with the *lately technique* . . .

> "Oh? What's been going fine lately?"
> "What's been good lately?"
> "What's been 'the usual' lately?"
> "What's been keeping you so busy lately?"

. . . . you invite a more detailed response that helps you get to know the other person's specific circumstances. From there you can transition into personalized questions.

Another simple approach to try is the *enjoy most* question, which prompts the conversation in a positive direction and applies to any of the WBT topics:

> Which season do you enjoy the most?
> Which part of your job do you enjoy most?
> Which of your travels did you enjoy most?

You can also apply the *enjoy most* question to the context of your meeting.

> What do you enjoy most about working from home?
> What do you enjoy most about your new role?
> What have you enjoyed most about the conference so far?

Follow these up with "why?" and you'll learn a great deal about the other person's preferences. You will probably discover some common ground, too.

Another way to make small talk more enjoyable is the *do for fun* technique. You can either ask them what they do for fun, or you can focus the question on how they spent their previous weekend (on a Monday or Tuesday) or how they plan to spend the upcoming one. Unless they work non-stop, they will likely share insights into their family life and leisure activities. This approach establishes a more personal, relatable connection and may reveal a few shared interests.

When we teach business development to large groups, we often receive questions from junior professionals intrigued by the Short List concept but concerned that they do not yet have clients to refer or connectors to introduce to the more influential people they would like to nurture. We encourage them not to sell themselves short. Use the *lately technique* to learn about the more established person you're getting to know. It invites them to share about the challenges that have been troubling them. Their complaint about their department could be an opportunity to broaden their thinking with a multi-generational perspective. The deadlines they're up against could be alleviated with a little innovation ("There's a new app that does that in a fraction of the time") or an introduction to a friend who is looking for a new job.

As you use the *do for fun, enjoy most,* or *lately technique* to learn about the people on your Short List and the details in their lives, you will discover commonalities that strengthen the relationship. Commonalities help us feel more related to one another. The more commonalities we share, the more trust and like-mindedness we experience. But in addition to these techniques, a small investment in preparation and forethought will pay off nicely. Before your next meeting with them, spend a few minutes on their social media accounts to see what they have been up to. Did they "like" an article on a recent development in their industry? Did they post pictures from a weekend volunteer activity? Are they encouraging donations for a charitable cause? Once you have this information, you can easily fill any pause with, "Oh, by the way, I noticed your LinkedIn post about the new hire. How does their addition to your firm help you?" This kind of personalized question spurs an exchange about a topic that is immediately relevant to them.

Of course, the more you get to know the people on your Short List, the more abundantly your conversations will flow. It will become second nature to ask about the status of that project that consumed their prior quarter, see how they are settling into their new house, or exchange details about your favorite summer getaways. But be wary of the tendency to backslide into generic conversation patterns during busy periods. It's human nature, especially when we are going through a particularly hectic time, to use WBT as a substitute for "catching up." I notice this tendency in myself on days when I have back-to-back meetings. Trying to be productive, I sometimes rush through the niceties so I can jump into my formal agenda. This approach may make for an efficient visit, but it also squanders an opportunity to reinforce my relationship with the other person. The fact is that it takes the same amount of time to chit-chat about the weather as it does to ask the other person a specific question about their work or personal life. When we are not mindful of this fact, we become lazy conversationalists, but when we show concern for the details that make up people's lives, our interactions become more purposeful. We create more substantial connections among our Short Lists, and they, in turn, become far more likely to reciprocate.

Exercise: Email Efficacy Test

 10–15 minutes

This exercise will put some of the email best practices in this chapter into action for you.

> Step 1: Open your email application and find the last five emails in your Sent folder that you delivered to prospects and other contacts you don't know particularly well.

Step 2: Notice the extent to which you applied the best practices in this chapter: using personalization in your opener and closing questions to conclude your message.

Step 3: Note if there were any correlations between the best practices and your response rate.

Step 4: Resend any of the messages that did not receive a response, only this time, personalize the opener and end with a closing question.

Step 5: Observe whether the best practices improve your response rate.

Scan this QR code to download a PDF of this exercise and the corresponding worksheets.

PART 4

Elevating Your Short List and Sustaining Momentum

Chapter 14

How to Activate Connectors

Connectors have access to information and business opportunities that can catalyze your success. A referral from a connector skips past the first three engagement stages. The prospect is ready to meet with you solely based on the recommendation from their trusted contact.

THE SEVEN STAGES OF ENGAGEMENT

Based on the actions a prospect, connector, or client take in their engagement journey.

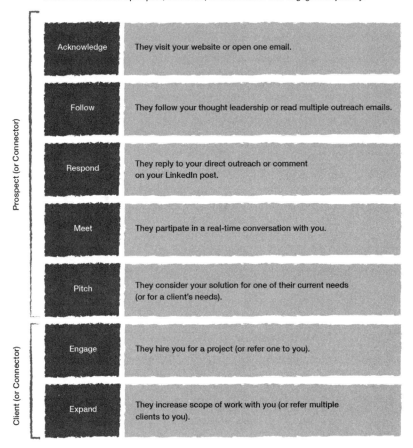

Acknowledge	They visit your website or open one email.
Follow	They follow your thought leadership or read multiple outreach emails.
Respond	They reply to your direct outreach or comment on your LinkedIn post.
Meet	They partipate in a real-time conversation with you.
Pitch	They consider your solution for one of their current needs (or for a client's needs).
Engage	They hire you for a project (or refer one to you).
Expand	They increase scope of work with you (or refer multiple clients to you).

Prospect (or Connector): Acknowledge, Follow, Respond, Meet, Pitch

Client (or Connector): Engage, Expand

SIX STEPS TO CONVERT CONNECTORS INTO CATALYSTS

Like any contact in your Short List, you must nurture your connectors if you expect to maximize their beneficial impact on your business. In this section of the book, I will walk you through the six steps that convert connectors into catalysts. (You're welcome, alliteration enthusiasts.) These steps are based on common sense and common courtesy, yet they are often ignored. Follow them, and you will capitalize on the many benefits your connectors are ready and willing to provide.

Step 1: Present your connectors with a connection request.

If you are following the guidelines in this book, your connectors possess the fourth C: collaboration. That means they are inclined toward helpfulness and have indicated that intention toward you. But unless they also happen to be mind readers, they will only know how to connect you with the right people and information if you tell them what you are looking for. A connection request removes any uncertainty they may have about how they can help.

Many of us hesitate when it comes to asking for help. We worry that if we make a request of another person, we will inconvenience them, or risk appearing helpless. Dr. Xuan Zhao, a social psychologist, researched this tendency while at the University of Chicago and published her findings in *Psychological Science*. She observed a persistent difference between how help-seekers and potential helpers view the same event. Help-seekers consistently underestimate how willing others are to help them and how positive the helpers felt afterward. In her studies, help-seekers overestimated how inconvenienced helpers would feel by a factor of up to 6x.[14]

Reflect on your own experience as a helper. Think about the last time you helped a friend or a client. Didn't it feel good? Weren't you ready and willing to help further? Personally, it gives me a sense of satisfaction to know I've made a positive difference in people's lives, especially those on my Short List. And yet, we all tend to assume it will land differently should we find ourselves on the receiving end of a good turn.

I see this play out often in meetings between connectors. They invest time getting to know one another, discover personal commonalities and professional synergies, but the closest they come to

---

14 Xuan Zhao and Nicholas Epley, "Surprisingly Happy to Have Helped: Underestimating Prosociality Creates a Misplaced Barrier to Asking for Help," *Psychological Science* 33(10), 2022, 1708–1731, https://doi.org/10.1177/09567976221097615.

actualizing their relationship is the all-too-common phrase at the end of the meeting: "keep me in mind."

> "Keep me in mind if you encounter anyone who could use my services, Jane."
> "Will do, Larry!"

The trouble is, even with the best of intentions, Jane will struggle to keep Larry's "keep me in mind" in mind. Its passive nature and lack of specificity ensures the request will fade into the background while Jane focuses on actionable priorities and concrete deadlines she can successfully accomplish. Larry would have been better off with an intentional approach, structuring his connection request with the same SMART framework he applied to his goals.

> Specific: Let your connector know exactly what you're trying to accomplish.
>
> Measurable: Define the parameters of your request.
>
> Actionable: "Keep me in mind" is passive, not actionable. Be direct.
>
> Realistic: Your request needs to be quick and painless to fulfill. Don't burden them with laborious homework. Make it easy for them to say yes to you.
>
> Time-bound: Busy people work with deadlines. Propose a reasonable timeline.

Here's how your introduction request might sound using the SMART framework:

"Chris, I'd like your help with something. I'm working on growing my book of business this year, and I'm interested in meeting at least three CFOs at middle-market biotech companies in the Washington, DC metro area." (Specific and measurable)

"I'd like to set up a time for us to sit down and brainstorm the CFO contacts in your network who you might be willing to introduce to me." (Actionable)

"To prepare for our meeting, I'll search your LinkedIn connections and flag the biotech CFOs in your network. That way we can review my selections and discuss whether an introduction makes sense based on your relationship with them and comfort level. In the spirit of reciprocity, I invite you to do the same with my LinkedIn connections—I'm sure I know a few people you'd like to meet too." (Realistic)

"Do you think you could make time for that exercise sometime next month?" (Time-bound)

According to Zhao, helpfulness also increases emotional closeness. Your connection request communicates that you are willing to let your guard down with your connector. It's a meaningful trust move, reserved for a select few, introducing a more intentional and productive dynamic to your relationship. It takes you one step closer to securing a place on *their* Short List. Here are a few personal examples of connection requests I made that paid off nicely.

Boosting the Pipeline

During the pandemic, our business took a turn for the worse. Confronting an uncertain economy and a disrupted marketplace, some of our clients put projects on hold until they could assess how *their* clients were going to proceed. As the CEO of my company, I was beside myself. We had enjoyed steady growth for nearly twenty years. I'd never experienced a sudden retraction like this before. I felt equal parts helpless and hopeless. Fortunately, my connectors came to my rescue.

I belong to a group of business leaders—we call ourselves the business forum. We meet monthly so we can stay connected, keep each other abreast of personal and business news, and support each other. I shared my predicament with them, along with a request to meet one-on-one so we could brainstorm introductions that would help turn things around for my company. Everyone in the group agreed to do so.

These conversations were incredibly encouraging to me. They reminded me that I was not alone, and that my network of connectors would rally when I needed them to. Within a few weeks, I was taking meetings with a host of new prospects, all introduced through my forum network.

Expanding into New Markets

A colleague and I from the PipelinePlus team recently flew to London to facilitate BD training for one of our clients: a global engineering consulting firm. I don't have a robust network in London, but I have a few people on my Short List who do, so I contacted them with this request: "I'm going to be in London on a business trip next month. While I'm in the city, I'd like to set up meetings with CMOs and business leaders at UK-based firms so I can better understand the marketplace and explore how we might be able to help one another. Do you have any contacts in London who you would feel comfortable making the introduction?" Within a couple of days, I had several London meetings scheduled with prospects and potential connectors, making my trip across the pond much more productive.

Growing Existing Initiatives

I facilitate several roundtables made up of managing partners from law firms. I saw an opportunity to grow one of the groups, so I put out a message to the members. "I'd like to add a few fresh perspectives to our group. Do any of you know managing partners from similarly situated law firms who would be a good fit for our group? If so, please share their names and firms with me so I can consider them for membership." Two introductions came back, and within a few weeks, we had a new member, referred by an existing one.

Step 2: After requesting an introduction, provide an assist.

In sports, an assist is an action a player takes to help another player score a goal. In business development, it's something you can provide that makes it easier for your connector to help you. Let's say you make a connection request for CEOs who plan to exit in the next few years, and your connector happens to know of one. Now comes the tricky part. If you respond with, "Great, please introduce me to your CEO friend," it puts your connector in a difficult position. After all, the CEO may not be interested in meeting with you, especially if your plan is to just pitch your services. Instead, give your connector an assist that piques the CEO's interest and makes it easier to introduce you.

Here's an example of an assist a corporate lawyer might use: "Thanks for offering to introduce me to your CEO friend. When you reach out to her, let her know that, in my experience as a corporate attorney, most business owners haven't properly prepared their business for sale, and as a result, the transaction ends up costing them a lot more time and money than they anticipate. I regularly take CEOs through a due diligence assessment that can save thousands in legal fees and can add significantly to the value of their exit. I'd be happy to walk your friend through my assessment at no charge."

This assist is a win all around. The connector gets to offer something of value to their CEO friend. The CEO gets a complimentary assessment that helps her business. And the attorney gets to share a relevant work sample with a prospect. If the CEO doesn't plan to sell her business, she'll likely let the connector know, and the corporate lawyer won't waste time pursuing a prospect who does not fit their ideal client profile.

As you think about your assist, consider your most recent clients. What events lead to their need for your services? What circumstances made it easy for them to engage you? Each of these can be fashioned into assists that make your connectors look good when they approach prospects on your behalf.

Step 3: When a connector sends you a prospect, keep them in the loop.

If the prospect doesn't return your call, your connector can nudge them. If the prospect doesn't immediately engage you, your connector can check in and give you a sense of their reservation. If the prospect does engage you, your connector can encourage and reinforce your new client's decision. In short, your connector can be an important collaborator in the process, but only if they know what transpired after they made the referral.

Here's an example of how this approach can play out in your favor:

"Ariel, I really appreciate your referral to Caroline, the CFO of ClearGroup. I followed up on your introduction over a week ago but haven't heard back. You mentioned that Caroline needs to act quickly on an audit. Would you mind checking in to make sure she received my message?"

The next day, Ariel gets back to you. "Hi Carlos. I spoke with Caroline. She appreciated your outreach, but she is concerned about fees given that you're at a bigger firm. She reached out to a small boutique a few days ago, but the proposal they sent her was confusing. The whole process is taking longer than she'd like given her encroaching deadline, but cost control is important to her."

"Thanks, Ariel. I understand. Please let Caroline know that we can present a few competitive options that should address both her budget and timing issues. If she gives me a call, I'll walk her through the details and we can get her what she needs by the end of the day."

By integrating your connector, this collaborative approach opened a line of communication that addressed the prospect's concerns, saving them wasted time and an engagement with a potentially less sophisticated competitor.

Step 4: After a connector sends you a prospect, thank them.

This is one of the most common reasons connectors stop connecting. They send a piece of business and never get thanked. The way you thank your connector is up to you. It could range from a quick text to a high-end dinner, depending on the lengths they went to, and the value of their contribution. Match your gesture to the situation but note that when people are appreciated for their act of kindness, they are more inclined to repeat the behavior in the future. Conversely, when they feel taken for granted, they're unlikely to help that person again.

Consider this scenario: A connector has a client who needs a good consultant. They know at least two people with the right expertise, so they refer both consultants. Consultant #1 responds immediately with a thoughtful, handwritten note thanking the connector for their help, and follows up a few days later with an update on how the meeting went. Consultant #2 does neither of these things. Who do you suppose the connector will favor when the next referral opportunity comes along?

Consultant #1's consideration and professionalism demonstrate how they conduct business. Their message is, "I am service-oriented, and I'm never too busy to take care of the relationships who take care of me." As for consultant #2, the connector is left to wonder if they are similarly noncommunicative with the prospect they were just referred to, or their own clients for that matter. Reward the goodwill you receive from your connectors so they shower you with more of it in the future.

Step 5: If you can't help the prospect, send them back to the referral source.

Here's the situation: Your connector sends you a prospect. After interviewing them, you assess that they aren't the right client for you, so you refer them to someone else. You may think you were being helpful, but you've just taken an opportunity from your connector. They might have had a second option they wanted to send their client to. They might have had a negative opinion about the person you referred. Remember, this isn't your relationship, it's theirs. So, allow them to control the process as they see fit. Be a thoughtful, respectful referral partner.

Step 6: Reciprocate whenever you can.

When a connector introduces you to someone, make an effort to reciprocate with an introduction of your own. If you can't think of a prospect for your connector, introduce them to other potential referral sources instead. A good connector can be even more valuable than a prospect.

ADVISORY ROUNDTABLES

Another way to activate connectors is through an advisory round-table. This mastermind forum allows you and your connectors to deepen your relationships, exchange valuable information, and boost referral activity.

An advisory roundtable is a carefully curated group of advisors who convene regularly for brainstorming and resource-sharing. The key objective is to bring together professionals from diverse but complementary disciplines such as law, accounting, finance, and consulting. This diversity ensures a wealth of perspectives and cross-referral potential, making each meeting a valuable experience for all participants.

The primary advantage of an advisory roundtable is to gain an outside perspective. Members look beyond their immediate professional spheres, broadening their understanding and insights. The intimate size of the group (preferably fewer than eight people) and regular cadence of meetings (preferably monthly) fosters deeper relationships, which inevitably leads to members with a genuine interest in helping each other personally and professionally.

To launch your advisory roundtable, follow these steps:

1. **Create the invitation.** Begin by writing out a clear and compelling invitation to join your advisory roundtable. You will use this message to recruit your first few members. Your invitation should clearly outline the objectives, benefits, and expectations for participants. For example:

   "I am putting together a group of select advisors from my network to meet regularly for collaborative discussions, resource-sharing, and mutual support. The goal is to share our diverse perspectives, enhance our professional insights, and create a productive referral network. I'd like you to be part of the founding team. If you're open to the idea, let's meet to discuss the idea further and launch the group together."

2. **Identify potential members.** Send the invitation to one or more connectors on your Short List. You may also consider inviting people in your broader network, assuming they fit your advisory roundtable profile: individuals who will not only benefit from the group but can also contribute actively to its success.

3. **Extend invitations.** Invite your potential members to join you for the first meeting. Let them know your reasoning for starting the roundtable, why you invited them to be part of the founding group, and how their participation will be mutually beneficial. Ask them what they would like to get out of the group, integrate their ideas, and brainstorm additional potential members to invite to your second meeting.

4. **Evolve.** It will take a few meetings for your advisory roundtable to take shape. Set clear parameters for participation, including

how many meetings a member needs to attend to remain in good standing with the group. Regular communication, respectful collaboration, and a commitment to follow through on shared objectives will be essential for success. Don't be surprised if a founding member phases out, or if an unexpected guest steps up. Those who resonate with the concept will self-identify and the group will settle into a productive rhythm.

5. **Formalize.** Advisory roundtables are only as effective as the commitment and engagement of their members. Poor leadership or insufficient structure can lead to the disintegration of the group. Ensure that you have a core group of individuals who are dedicated to attending meetings, actively participating, communicating respectfully, and fulfilling their commitments.

By following these steps and maintaining a focus on active participation and commitment, you can harness the power of advisory roundtables to transform your connectors into catalysts. This model deepens relationships and significantly amplifies referral activity. It also surfaces new connectors for your Short List and enables you to efficiently interact with several important people in your network. It is a time-saver, a network-builder, and a relationship-amplifier.

NURTURING EXTERNAL MENTORS

A mentor is a unique breed of connector, not to be overlooked as you activate key people on your Short List. When most people think of mentorship, they assume it is reserved for the early stages of one's career. Au contraire! I am a veteran business developer and CEO, and I maintain several mentors in my Short List. These connectors advise me in areas where I want to learn more or expand into new industries. Granted, I don't necessarily refer to them as mentors (some of them are uncomfortable with such formalities), but nevertheless they broaden my perspective, and my world is all the richer for it.

In my experience, knowledge is power, and mentorship is a key conduit to accessing that power. Looking to scale up your book of business? You'll need a business development mentor. Transitioning from mid-career into a leadership role? You'll need a leadership mentor. Intending to expand into a new industry? You'd benefit from a mentor who happens to be an industry leader. Looking to nurture a team so you can leverage your workload into a more profitable model? You'll need to become a mentor.

If you work at a firm, you've probably experienced mentorship. Internal mentors often impart technical expertise so you can deliver better client service, but they rarely hand over a prospect to improve your client development. They're saving those opportunities for their own books of business. That's why when we coach people, we recommend they seek out external mentors—people outside their firm—who can guide them through challenges and open doors to new opportunities. An external mentor might be a business leader, industry expert, or decision-maker with a helpful disposition.

Steps for Securing and Benefiting from a Mentor

Follow these four steps to secure an external mentor and turn them into a career booster:

1. **Identify the mentor.** A good candidate will have the following observable characteristics:

   - They are in a position to help you. For instance, they may run their own company, sit on a board of directors for a major institution in your industry, or serve as a leader in your business community.

- They share commonalities with you. Perhaps they grew up in your hometown or attended your alma mater. Even shared interests can be an effective point of entry to establish a connection.

- They have sufficient life experience to contribute meaningful advice and resources. Their accomplishments should seem impressive to you. (It's okay to be a little jealous.)

2. **Approach the mentor.** Once you have identified your candidate, send them a message. (If you don't have their email address, a LinkedIn direct message will do just fine.) Let them know why you are reaching out to them. Reference your shared commonalities and ask them if they would be willing to meet with you so you can seek their advice on a topic for which you feel they are uniquely qualified. Make it easy for them to agree to your request. The meeting should be virtual. The timeframe should be at their convenience. The amount of time you ask for should be no more than fifteen minutes. (If the two of you hit it off, they will probably give you more time.)

3. **The first meeting.** When you meet with them, let them know your SMART goals and reiterate why their perspective is relevant to what you're trying to accomplish. Then, ask them what they would do if they were in your shoes. Assuming the meeting goes well, let them know that you will follow up with them as soon as you have applied their advice. This last piece is important. It sets the expectation that your outreach wasn't just a "can I pick your brain" one-off. It implies that the two of you may enjoy a sustained mentorship.

4. **The next few meetings.** Whenever you employ their advice, let them know how it was helpful. Tell them exactly what you learned from their mentorship and thank them for their

guidance. Share your successes with them so that they experience the pride and personal satisfaction that comes with mentoring. Then, when you encounter your next challenge, suggest that the two of you get together again to discuss.

The right mentor will help to round out your professional development and business acumen. As your relationship matures, they will become invested in your advancement and will begin to facilitate powerful introductions that could otherwise take at least a decade to access through organic networking. They will invite you to functions that some of the most established partners at your firm can't get in to. In time, they will become a valuable part of your Short List, and your success.

Giving Back to Your Mentor

After a few visits to the well, you might start to feel indebted to your external mentors and think, "They give and I take. What could I possibly give back that they would want?" Don't forget that you're providing them with an opportunity to be helpful. For many mentors, that is reward enough. Also, as you get to know them, you will learn about the people they care about. Perhaps you can help one of them. Maybe they have a nephew who is looking for their first job and you can put in a good word for them at your firm. Or perhaps their daughter is applying to your alma mater and would benefit from an alumni interview. When you do something for someone your mentor cares about, it carries even more value than helping them directly.

Finally, don't forget to do some mentoring of your own. Help advance the careers of the people who look up to you. It's not only a source of personal satisfaction, but it is also an investment in your future. In today's dynamic business landscape, it's only a matter of time before one of your mentees transitions into a new role and becomes a prospect.

Exercise: Complete the Connector Catalyst Worksheet

 5–10 minutes

This exercise helps you quickly analyze your most productive connectors, brainstorm how you can incentivize them to contribute even more, and think about where to find others just like them.

	List your medium- and high-value clients.	Name the connector who made the referral or helped you secure the client.
1.		
2.		
3.		
4.		
5.		
6.		
7.		
8.		
9.		
10.		

Name the connectors who refer the most business.	How did you meet them?
1.	
2.	
3.	

What actions can you take to incentivize more business from your high-value connectors? (Review the list of Forty Actions at http://www.pipelineplus.com/theshortlist for ideas)	
1.
2.
3.

What actions can you take to add more high-value connectors to your Short List?
1.
2.
3.

Scan this QR code to download a PDF of this exercise and the corresponding worksheets.

Chapter 15

How to Convert Prospects into Clients: The Pitch

In professional services, individuals typically navigate the initial four stages of the engagement process—acknowledge, follow, respond, and meet—relatively easily.

These stages revolve around familiar principles like being helpful and delivering valuable information, which are standard practices in client service.

THE SEVEN STAGES OF ENGAGEMENT

Based on the actions a prospect, connector, or client take in their engagement journey.

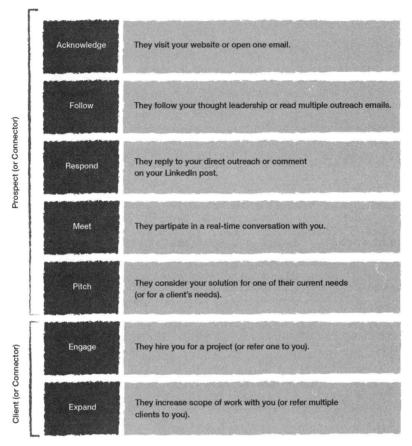

Prospect (or Connector)

Acknowledge	They visit your website or open one email.
Follow	They follow your thought leadership or read multiple outreach emails.
Respond	They reply to your direct outreach or comment on your LinkedIn post.
Meet	They partipate in a real-time conversation with you.
Pitch	They consider your solution for one of their current needs (or for a client's needs).

Client (or Connector)

Engage	They hire you for a project (or refer one to you).
Expand	They increase scope of work with you (or refer multiple clients to you).

But the pitch stage poses a distinct challenge. It demands skills that are uneasy for many, such as selling, negotiating, and, at times, directly asking for business.

TURNING FRIENDS INTO CLIENTS

The pitch stage can be particularly tricky when the prospect is in your personal network. We all find ourselves in that precarious position from time to time: We learn that a longtime friend or relative is either a prospective client or has access to one, but we don't broach the subject of business for fear of introducing awkwardness into the relationship. So, we console ourselves with narratives like, "They know what I do for a living, and they will let me know if they need my help." But such assumptions prove to be frustratingly inaccurate when we learn that they've engaged or referred a competitor for reasons that are difficult to fathom and awkward to explore.

Often, our reluctance to broach a business topic with a friend has to do with the fact that we are unsure as to the status of the relationship. According to extensive social experiments conducted jointly in 2016 by Tel Aviv University and MIT,[15] 95 percent of people believe their friendships are reciprocal when in truth, only half of them are. We are often disappointed by people whose loyalty fails to meet our expectations. We also find ourselves backing away from people whose expectations of a mutual friendship do not match our feelings for them. A need-to-have on one side of a relationship is often matched to a nice-to-have on the other side, which is why it's important to approach a business dialogue with a friend from an exploratory position rather than a presumptive one.

These informal approaches explore the business potential of your personal contacts in an easy, conversational manner:

- **Ask about their work life.** It may seem obvious, but we tend to gloss over this topic with friends and relatives, thereby missing an opportunity to understand their business needs. Express the same level of concern for their professional health as you would their physical or emotional well-being. One way to do this is to ask, "How are things at work?" Use the *lately technique* if their response is vague or generic. Once you

---

15   Abdullah Almaatouq, Laura Radaelli, Alex Pentland, and Erez Shmueli, "Are You Your Friends' Friend? Poor Perception of Friendship Ties Limits the Ability to Promote Behavioral Change," *PLOS One*, 11(3), March 22, 2016, https://doi.org/10.1371/journal.pone.0151588.

have a better sense of their business challenges, you can offer a helping hand.

- **Share about your work life.** One of the first questions our friends ask when we see them is, "How are things going?" or "How's business?" If you want your friend to understand what you do and how it might be relevant to their needs, take the opportunity to provide a genuine answer to their question. Fill them in on your latest win. Tell the story of how satisfying it was when you recently solved a particularly complex problem for a client. Let them know how important your work is to you. Sharing professional details may not translate into business from your friend in the short term, but it will help them understand you better and introduce a broader landscape of work-related topics for further exploration.

- **Ask for their consideration.** Let them know your SMART goals, and the kinds of people you are trying to meet so they can keep an eye out for you. Given your friendship, they will likely be invested in your success and willing to offer helpful suggestions and introductions.

- **Be transparent.** Tell your friend you've been wanting to ask them if you could be of assistance in a professional context but put it off for fear of seeming inappropriate. If they agree with your initial impulse, respect their preferences and move on to another topic. If they tell you to stop overthinking, go ahead and have the conversation you've denied each other.

Of course, before you launch into any of these approaches, consider your audience. Every friendship is unique. Perhaps your friend prefers to compartmentalize their life so that personal relationships are separate from professional ones. In that case, ease in and be prepared to back off. It may take time before they become comfortable with the idea of mixing business with pleasure. But don't give up. Eventually, these approaches will introduce work-related topics into your dialogues so that your friends begin to think of you as someone with whom they can discuss business issues. It may start with a casual request for your professional advice or a more relaxed reaction when you ask for theirs.

It's ironic that the people who make us feel the most comfortable in life are often the clumsiest to engage in a conversation about business development. And indeed, we all have relationships that are best left as they are. But with a bit of forethought, creativity, and proactivity, you can initiate a comfortable dialogue with many of your closest relationships and explore your interest in helping one another.

INITIAL CONSULTATIONS WITH PROSPECTS

Whether shopping for a scoop of ice cream, a software program, or a new service provider, it is reasonable for a prospect to expect a free sample or trial before committing to a purchase. In the context of professional services, the initial consultation allows the prospect to experience your expertise firsthand, establish trust, and make an informed decision. But the initial consultation is also an opportunity for you to do some vetting of your own.

If a connector referred the prospect to you, get as many details as possible before the consultation meeting. How does the connector know the prospect? What did the prospect share with them about their problem? Did the connector provide your name only, or multiple options for the prospect to interview? Also, conduct an online pre-screen to ensure the prospect fits your ideal client profile. You can delegate this task to your assistant, who can call ahead and ask vetting questions such as, "Help us understand the nature of the problem you wish to discuss so we can best prepare for the consultation meeting." This step minimizes the time you might otherwise spend with a prospect who isn't a fit for your business.

Your assistant can also provide advanced research on the prospect's company by exploring their website, taking note of the number of employees they have, and delving into their LinkedIn profiles to gauge their sophistication as buyers. For larger companies, a review of their D&B (Dunn & Bradstreet) or 10-K information can help you confirm whether the prospect is appropriately high-value and deserving of your initial complimentary meeting.

Armed with the insights gathered during pre-screening and online research, you can tailor your approach for the initial consultation. This personalized touch demonstrates your commitment to understanding their unique needs and positions you as the kind of advisor who invests in client success.

PROPOSALS

If your industry frequently uses RFPs to vet providers, you can gain access to the middle of a prospect's engagement process. Their RFP (request for proposal) invites a pitch from qualified firms, regardless of whether the prospect previously acknowledged, followed, or responded to your outreach. Certainly, firms who engage with prospects beforehand hold a much stronger position in the RFP process, but some firms invest very little energy in building relationships, relying solely on RFPs to secure new work.

Writing, submitting, tracking, and winning work through proposals can be very labor intensive, so it's crucial to put a well-defined go/no-go process in place so you only pursue the ones with the highest chances of success. Your go/no-go process consists of qualifiers that allow you to evaluate opportunities based on their alignment with your strengths, capabilities, and the likelihood of success. Examples might include:

- Does this RFP present the kind of opportunity we typically win?

- Does the scope of services align with our firm's strengths?

- Does the profitability of the work outlined in the RFP outweigh the opportunity cost of pursuing it?

- Do we have the time and resources to prepare a strong response?

- Which competitors are also likely to submit a proposal, and do our proposals historically win over theirs?

If enough of the answers to these questions are "no," the RFP is a no-go. Pursuing a no-go has a low chance of success and will likely reduce your win rate.

Assuming the RFP is a "go," and you invest time creating the document, request a review meeting with a client contact to go over the proposal before submitting it. This meeting ensures you meet the client's satisfaction requirements and confirms that your fee structure aligns with their expectations. It also allows you to ask questions about their approval process. Who are the decision-makers? What are their priorities? Will there be an opportunity to present your proposal to them and answer their questions directly? (Whenever one of our prospects agrees to a proposal-review meeting, they typically request edits that strengthen our proposals and provide useful information about the decision process.)

Requesting a proposal-review meeting may seem counterintuitive, especially in scenarios that involve procurement or restricted communication. But it never hurts to ask for the proposal-review meeting. Let your competitors be the ones who assume it isn't available to them.

It's also important to realize that in the world of proposals, not every request is genuine. Sometimes prospects ask for a proposal just to avoid further conversations. Sometimes, they have the best purchasing intentions but become distracted by other priorities. Track the open links in your proposals to gauge engagement and add the open rate metric to your win rate analysis.

If you find that you are dealing exclusively with gatekeepers and have no access to the decision-makers, ask for the names of those making the final determination and take these three steps:

1. Share relevant case studies or support materials and request that the gatekeepers pass them along to decision-makers.

2. Connect with decision-makers on LinkedIn with a personalized note. Reference the gatekeepers you've been talking to and thank the decision-makers for the opportunity to be considered. Then, follow and support any posts they make on LinkedIn. This approach is a courteous gesture and gets you onto their radar.

3. Extend invitations for upcoming presentations or webinars and include them in any relevant publication announcements so they have a sense of your presence as a thought leader in the marketplace.

This goes without saying, but do not go over your gatekeeper's head and try to pitch the decision-maker.

An effective proposal process involves more than just creating compelling documents; it requires a strategy for prioritizing the right opportunities, an information-gathering exercise with the gatekeepers, and a proactive touchpoint with the decision-makers. These combined steps help to strengthen your position against competitors gunning for the same work.

PITCH MEETINGS

Unlike a casual exploration with a friend, a formal pitch meeting is a dedicated conversation oriented around a buying opportunity. It is usually held with a new prospect, though the same process applies when pitching a client on the idea of expanding the scope of provided services. A pitch meeting typically consists of five distinct parts, each contributing to a successful outcome.

Build Rapport

Every meeting begins with small talk. For some, it is perfunctory chit-chat. For others, it is a significant opportunity to get comfortable and build rapport. A strong rapport goes a long way toward a successful outcome at a pitch meeting. According to research conducted by the Artemis Partnership and profiled in Bob Wiesner's book, *Winning Is Better*, B2B buyers award wins based on relationships 72 percent of the time. That's why targeting and developing solid relationships with prospects is worth the effort.

But when a pitch meeting comes to you through a formal RFP or a referral, you may find yourself pitching prospects you're only meeting for the first time. In these instances, research them online before the meeting. What commonalities can you reference in their LinkedIn profile, social media posts, blogs, podcast interviews, or articles? Did you go to the same schools? Do you share their perspective on industry issues? Which of the developments in their press releases would you like to know more about? What recent industry trends are you curious to know their perspectives on? Prepare a few questions you can ask at the top of the pitch meeting to elevate the conversation beyond generic small talk.

During the meeting, eliminate distractions by turning off your mobile devices. Place them out of sight so your prospect understands you intend to give them your full attention. Take your time in building rapport; don't rush the conversation. Let the prospect shorten or extend the rapport-building phase according to their timetable, comfort, and readiness to delve into the business discussion. They may need to assess their affinity with you; they may have a strong preference for initial small talk. Follow their lead so that you progress to the next stage only when they're ready to discuss their problem with you.

Understand Their Problem

Your clients do not have sufficient expertise to solve many of their problems. If they did, they would not need to schedule pitch meetings with outside experts. Of course, you are the expert in solving the kinds of problems your *clients* have. But it's important to remember that you are not the expert when it comes to the nuances of the specific problems your *prospects* have. There are unique circumstances in their situation that you must explore and fully understand before your pitch will resonate. Only through genuine curiosity about their situation will you be able to design a bespoke solution that stands apart from the competition.

Your prospect will expect that you have questions about their situation, but they will also expect that you've done your due diligence. If you ask them about information readily available online, you come across as unprepared. That's why we recommend that you begin by establishing your relevant knowledge. You can do this simply by saying, "Here's what we know," followed by a review of the conditions in the RFP, any information you may have received from the person who referred the opportunity, and the online research you conducted when you prepared for the pitch meeting. Once you've outlined their problem as you understand it, look to the prospect for clarification by asking, "What else should we know?"

This open-ended question prompts your prospect to fill in any gaps in your assessment of their situation. Perhaps a new piece of information has come to light. There may be a cultural or political nuance that only those inside the company know, which you should integrate into your proposed solution.

The "Here's what we know, what else should we know" approach provides a framework to explore the prospect's problems during a formal pitch. Still, suppose you find yourself in a more informal conversation, where the prospect's background information is limited (like a lunch with a friend who happens to be a decision-maker at their company or an introductory meeting with a prospect who is trying to ascertain their interest in your services). In that case, the prospect may ask you a general question like, "So, how do you help your clients?" Your best move in this instance is to defer your answer until you fully understand the prospect's problem. You can do this by saying, "I'm happy to tell you how we help our clients, but first, I'd like to get a better sense of your needs so that my response is relevant. Can you tell me a little more about your situation?" They will let you take the lead if you ask for it respectfully, especially when the result will be a more informed sense of how you can help them.

Now that you're asking the questions, you can explore their challenges. Initially, they may start off with a general reason for their meeting with you. "We need assistance with our legal work," or "We need help implementing a project," or "I want to sell my company." If you immediately reply with a description of your relevant expertise, you only address their problem at a cosmetic level, and you sound like any competitor the prospect may be interviewing. But if you ask effective probing questions, you arm yourself with the information you'll need to understand the prospect's motivations, expectations, and success criteria.

Probing questions:

> **"Let's say we have the opportunity to work together. What outcomes are you hoping for?"**

This question invites your prospect to share their expectations and gives you a clear understanding of what success looks like in their minds. Tailor your proposed solution around their response.

> **"What other parts of the business are potentially impacted by this problem?"**

Use this as a launch point to explore the breadth of the problem's impact on other departments, initiatives, products, services, or strategies. The better you understand the implications of the problem, the better you will be able to look ahead and anticipate related issues that the prospect may have overlooked. A deeper understanding of the business will also identify cross-selling opportunities.

> **"Why are you prioritizing this problem now?"**

The answer to this question may be obvious if it's tied to a deadline or business imperative. Still, if the project in question could conceivably be deferred, this probing question helps you understand the circumstances driving the client's urgency. Why not put this off until next year? Why not insource the solution to an internal team instead of paying an outsourced provider? When you understand the client's motivation for taking immediate action, you gain an essential insight into their business priorities.

"What is *your* biggest challenge with respect to this problem?"

Your prospect's answer will reveal the aspect of the problem that most concerns them personally and the topic you should focus on when you start pitching your solution.

"Do you currently have a provider in this area? If so, why are you considering a change?"

Assuming the prospect is serious about switching firms, their response may give you some insight into their issues with their current provider. Perhaps they have had an unfavorable outcome or are frustrated with the lack of responsiveness or expertise. Perhaps the prospect has outgrown the incumbent provider. In any case, seek to understand the degree to which this plays into their stated problem.

Over time, you will develop other probing questions to ask your prospects during a pitch. And the more robust the rapport you build

at the outset of the meeting, the more information your prospect
will share when you ask your probing questions.

Propose Your Solution

Once you receive answers to your probing questions and better understand the prospect's problem, you can tell them how you intend to
help. For your solution to be compelling, it must do three things:

1. It must be informed.

2. It must demonstrate value.

3. It must be convincing.

Your Solution Must Be Informed

The difference between a good pitch and a great one often comes
down to the preparation that preceded the meeting. As you present
your solution, look for opportunities to reference your preliminary
research about the prospect's background or circumstances. Cite an
industry trend related to their situation or reference a relevant fact
you learned about the prospect's top competitor. A well-researched
solution bolsters your credibility in the prospect's mind and demonstrates the extent to which you are already informed about their
situation. It also compromises any competitor who couldn't find the
time to prepare their pitch as thoroughly as you did.

Your solution should also integrate the responses you received
from your prospect during your probing questions in the prior stage
of your pitch, but make sure to use the exact words they did to
describe their problem. Sometimes, in an effort to showcase expertise, a business developer will restate the prospect's problem in what
they believe to be more sophisticated, technical terms. But doing
so is like correcting them and can erode any rapport you built at

the outset of the meeting. When you restate the problem, favor the prospect's jargon over your own. This signals that you were listening carefully to their characterization, that you genuinely understand the situation from their perspective, and that their point of view informs your solution.

Your Solution Must Demonstrate Value

Take a consultative approach during your pitch. Act as if the prospect has already hired you and provide your best advice. Don't hold back, reserving your more salient points until they engage you. Remember, if they could solve this problem on their own, they already would have done so. Impress the prospect with your willingness to be of exceptional assistance such that they would be foolish not to include you among their circle of key advisors.

Also, to demonstrate value, look for ways to explain how you will deliver a return on the prospect's investment in your solution. This may not be immediately apparent. Most professional services are viewed as cost centers rather than profit centers. At the very least, tie your solution to one of the four reductions; help your prospect understand how your solution will reduce Risk, Inefficiency, Stress, or Expense. (We use the acronym RISE to help our clients remember the four reductions.) Prospects regularly engage providers who can alleviate these pain points, and if your solution addresses more than one of the four reductions, even better.

Your Solution Must Be Convincing

One of the most effective ways to ensure your solution is convincing is by referencing clients who benefited from your services in the past. Look to integrate case studies that involve similar problems you worked on, the solutions you provided, and the results they produced for the client. If appropriate, volunteer the clients in your case study as references so the prospect can speak to a few third parties about the outcomes you facilitated in the past.

Finally, look for opportunities to demonstrate the relevance of your solution in your follow-up to the meeting. If your prospect references attention to detail as an essential requirement, send them a detailed summary of the meeting when you return to your desk. If industry expertise is their primary concern, send them your best industry research piece as an example. If they indicate that responsiveness is important to them, don't just assure them in your pitch that you will be responsive. Ask them about their specific expectations for communication turnaround, and send your follow-up email within twenty-four hours, as implied.

Address Their Objections

A discerning prospect will likely have a few concerns, even after being presented with a compelling solution. Your first challenge is getting your prospect to voice any objections they may harbor. If they have a non-confrontational disposition, they may not volunteer their thoughts. They may nod and say, "This is all very interesting. Give us a few days to think about it." You leave the meeting under the impression that you are about to sign on a new client. By the time you learn that the work went to someone else, it's too late to explore or address the prospect's concerns. The best time to do that was during your pitch meeting.

So, after you've established rapport, explored the prospect's problem, and proposed your solution, use one of the following objection questions to field any potential concerns:

- Do you have any questions about how our proposed solution will solve your problem?

- Now that you've heard our proposed solution, is there anything you would like us to add or change?

- Do you have any concerns at this juncture that might keep us from working together?

As you listen to your prospect's response, you will find that their objections generally fall into one of three categories: ambiguity, fees, or firm.

Ambiguity

The most frustrating objection is ambiguity. Your prospect may be ready to discuss their challenges, but it doesn't mean they are ready to commit to a solution. Their hesitation could stem from uncertainty, a general aversion to change, or a lack of clarity about their needs. It's possible that they're just exploring options without a budget or a clear intention to engage a provider. This often happens when gatekeepers browse the marketplace for solutions without a timeline or preapproved budget from decision-makers. Based on my experience, in the rare cases when these prospects do progress to the next stage, the process tends to be especially lengthy.

Fees

If your prospect has an issue with your fees, you need to gain a better understanding of their budget and the monetary amount they expect a solution like yours should cost. Sometimes, it is in the prospect's nature to push for a discount no matter what fee you quote. But more likely, your prospect has not anticipated or budgeted for your proposed scope. You may have to negotiate with the prospect during the pitch meeting, so they don't disqualify you based on the assumption that you are too expensive for them. As a rule, you should always be prepared to present alternative fee arrangements that provide the flexibility fee-sensitive prospects will require to stay in dialogue with you. Remember that discounting is the most inferior alternative fee arrangement. You will learn negotiating techniques that empower you with more sophisticated, win-win options later in this section of the book.

Firm

The prospect may indicate unease with your firm by saying something like, "We're going to continue exploring other options," or "I'm not sure this is the right fit for our needs." That's your cue to learn more about their needs. Perhaps your probing questions failed to surface the real reason they agreed to meet with you. Maybe they felt your solution was too generic and lacked the required depth of expertise. Perhaps they disagree with your approach and prefer the solution one of your competitors pitched.

Use your remaining time in the meeting to focus on the disconnect between your solution and their problem. You can do this by saying, "It sounds like we should amend our approach. What kind of solution do you envision will work best for you?" This question invites the prospect to describe a situation you can potentially pivot into. If they mention they are already in dialogue with a competitor, tread carefully. Certainly, you can share information that differentiates you from another provider, but don't throw them under the bus in the process. Disparaging a competitor shows weak character and often backfires on the offending party.

In fact, it is essential to be gracious when you discuss *any* of the prospect's objections. Don't take their pushback personally. Resist the urge to become defensive or condescending. The prospect may indeed be making a short-sighted decision, or they may not know exactly what they want, but keep in mind that even if this pitch doesn't go your way, there may be a better opportunity to revisit the prospect's needs in the future. Regardless of the direction the pitch meeting takes, make sure the door is still open to you when it adjourns.

Ask for Their Business: The Close

The final step of a pitch meeting helps the prospect to make a clear decision and brings closure to the buying process. First, understand that an ethical closing technique never manipulates or pressures a prospect into engaging you. Your job leading up to the close is to ensure that the prospect understands how you can help, is unfettered by concerns, and can make a clear decision about whether or not to hire you. The close presents them with the opportunity to make that determination in the pitch meeting. It eliminates wasteful, meandering explorations that can drag on long after the pitch has concluded with no clear outcome.

Once you build rapport, understand their problem, propose your solution, and address their objections, invite the buyer to make a clear, informed decision about how they wish to proceed using one of the following closing techniques.

The Helpful Close

"Given our discussion today, how can I be of assistance to you?" This subtle close moves the pitch into its final stage and invites the prospect to direct the next action. It is intentionally open-ended so that the prospect can either suggest a minor advance, "I'd like you to meet my business partner," or a more significant one, "Great, let's get started." Of course, they may respond with something like, "I'm not yet sure how you can help," at which point you should come back to the objection questions and find out whether their hesitation is related to fees, firm, or something else.

The Collaborative Close

"What steps shall we take toward working together?" This close is more directed than the prior one, implying that you and the prospect are already a team partnering toward a common goal. It steers the conversation toward a series of actions both parties can take for mutual benefit. If the prospect expresses apprehension with a response like, "I'll need some time to think it over," or "I'm not sure . . ." it's likely that they are still harboring an objection.

The Hypothetical Close

"If you decide to work with us, here's what you can expect . . ." This close allows you to set the stage for subsequent steps, including the intake process, introductions to the client service team, the kickoff meeting, and your first set of deliverables. When you walk your prospect through this process, you set their expectations and help them envision the seamless experience of becoming your client.

The Silent Close

Your pitch likely includes a lot of new information for your prospect to process. When you observe that your prospect is considering your proposed solution seriously, stop talking for a few moments and give them time to think through your offering. Because a pitch is a high-stakes conversation, business developers often become excited and dominate the meeting by talking too much. Instead, slow your pace so the prospect has time to breathe, weigh their options, and ask a few clarifying questions. The silent close communicates your confidence and gravitas. It demonstrates that you have no intention of fast-talking or pressuring the prospect. If the silence becomes awkward, you can always propose the collaborative close or the hypothetical close. But it's just as likely that the prospect will break the silence with, "So, what's our next step?" That's your cue that they're ready to start working with you.

The Ask Close

"I'm looking forward to working with you. Shall we get started?" The ask close is an authentic, straightforward expression of your interest in a client relationship with the prospect. It is warranted when pitching a decision-maker who has already signaled that they want to work with you. While it is only practical in a pitch meeting to ask for the business, this technique is underutilized by many who fear that they will seem overly forward if they are transparent about their desire for the work. But the fact is, the ask close is nothing more than a question, and if you've prepared and delivered an effective pitch, your prospect's answer will probably be "yes."

The Advice Close

In the context of a formal, institutional pitch, you cannot prompt a buying decision during the meeting. The prospect will select a provider only after interviewing all competitors invited to pitch for the work in the RFP. But you can apply the advice close. Let's say you've presented your solution, which includes a unique area of expertise or some other characteristic that sets your firm apart. Before concluding the meeting, remind the prospect why your differentiator will be crucial to their success and advise them to consider only firms that can confidently deliver in that regard. Even though you have a bias, if your advice is sound, your advice close will work against competitors who do not emphasize your unique offering in their pitch.

Adapting to the Situation

The preceding techniques are effective whether in person or virtual. As you hone your pitching skills, you will select the appropriate close based on the forum of the meeting, the culture of the organization, the urgency of the prospect's needs, and your relationship with the prospect. This last point is especially relevant when pitching an institution. Your chances of success will be much higher if you have a champion within the organization who will look out for your interests in advance of, during, and after your pitch.

Also, keep in mind that every pitch meeting is different. While the typical flow will start with building rapport, followed by questions that help you understand their problem, your proposed solution, addressing their objections, and the close, it may play out in a different order. You may encounter a prospect with no initial interest in building rapport. They start the meeting with, "So, let's get down to business. How do you propose to solve our problem?" After getting only a cursory sense of your approach, they start flagging objections. Don't panic. The pitch meeting is off course, but you can still turn things around. Address their concerns and pivot back to your probing questions that put you back in the driver's seat. Your prospect may be more open to rapport building at the end of the meeting after you have impressed them with a thoughtful solution, informed by your smart questions. The more practiced you become at the pitch, the less disoriented you will be when your prospect throws a curve ball.

The Follow-Up

After you've concluded your close, express your enthusiasm for working with the prospect and clarify the steps you will be taking by way of follow-up. Notice whether the prospect reacts with a continuation or an advance. This terminology comes from Neil Rackham, who is best known for his book *SPIN Selling*. In the book, he describes a continuation as a communication where the prospect avoids taking a specific action. For example, they might say something like, "Let's stay in touch," or "Why don't you visit us next time you're in the area." Continuations typically signal that the prospect does not intend to engage you. An advance is a specific commitment that furthers the engagement. Rackham references examples like a concrete next step that involves both parties, the prospect's agreement to attend a follow-up meeting, or their plans to include other decision-makers and influencers who will weigh in on the buying decision. Of course, the optimal advance is their request to formalize a client relationship.

But sometimes, even an advance requires that you play the waiting game. Let's say your pitch meeting went well. You established rapport, identified the prospect's problem, pitched a compelling solution, addressed their objections, and presented a close that resonated well. They said they were very interested and would let you know their final decision soon. But it's been a month, and still no word.

This scenario often occurs when the prospect contemplates a new business strategy or a change in providers. Sometimes, they're just browsing, but they usually set up pitch meetings to find the right firm for their need. Then, the need changes. Perhaps their problem became less urgent, or one of their competitors signaled a move that altered their strategy. They may have realized they could forestall their decision to outsource for a few months if they made a new internal hire. They may be dealing with an internal stalemate between decision-makers, vendor champions, or departmental budget influencers. If your prospect is an individual or entrepreneur, they may simply be dragging their feet.

Unfortunately, prospects often don't communicate the details around their reservations, and too few firms ask for post-pitch feedback. They fall into the assumption trap, with justifications like:

- They're just busy, but I am top of mind for them.

- They will call when they are ready.

- I will seem desperate if I contact them.

- I'm too busy to follow up now, but I'll have more time later.

As far as you know, none of these things are true, but the assumptions are a convenient consolation when neither side is being proactive. An effective follow-up strategy replaces assumptions with action, giving you more influence over the outcome.

If the prospect is not responding to you, it is likely that they are focused on higher priority matters. Reminding them that they haven't gotten back to you doesn't add value to them. Instead, refer to the Forty Actions Matrix and start delivering value. Impress your prospect with your low-pressure, client-centric mindset. Make every interaction positive so it's easy for them to continue a dialogue with you. Treat the follow-up as an audition, during which you demonstrate your attentiveness, thoughtfulness, and professionalism.

A face-to-face follow-up is almost always more effective than a written one, so for local prospects who work in an office environment, arrange to "be in the neighborhood." Your message might sound like this: "I have a meeting around the corner from your building next week. Why don't I stop by for a quick cup of coffee so we can walk through the checklist I've prepared for you." A face-to-face meeting reinforces the relationship and allows the discussion to evolve more easily to other relevant topics. You can also propose the same technique as a videoconference if that's more convenient for them.

Deliver value-added follow-ups as frequently as possible. You won't have to worry about being a nuisance if you provide something helpful every time you contact them. And don't be discouraged if they are dismissive or unresponsive. Stay the course. Keep adding value. Before long, you will find that your value-added approach elevates your relationship with the prospect and helps you earn the right to broach unfinished business without putting a strain on the relationship. It also keeps you top of mind so that when it's finally time for them to decide, you are first in line.

However, even with this strategy, you may learn that the prospect chooses not to move forward with the project or engages another firm. That doesn't mean the door is closed to you forever. Consider that "no" means "not at this moment, but I might be interested later," so don't take it personally. They may fall off your Short List for the time being, but if you stay in their good graces, you will be in a stronger position to pitch again when your prospect switches roles or companies. Remember, your prospect is not just a stepping-stone to your next engagement. They represent a series of opportunities to be of service and deepen a client-side relationship.

Exercise: Develop Your Follow-Up Strategy

 10–15 minutes

This exercise will help you create a personalized follow-up strategy to maintain engagement with a prospect.

Step 1: Identify the Prospect

Select a prospect you have recently pitched or are planning to pitch.

Step 2: Research the Prospect

Find at least two new pieces of information about the prospect that you didn't already know, such as an industry trend, business challenge, or competitor action.

Step 3: Execute Your Follow-Up Strategy

Take a specific value-added action that is tied to the two pieces of information you discovered in your research. (For example, share an article that relates to their most recent LinkedIn post or something their biggest competitor is doing.)

Step 4: Reflect

Notice whether your follow-up strategy helped advance your opportunity. If not, consider how you might improve it in the future.

Scan this QR code to download a PDF of this exercise and the corresponding worksheets.

Chapter 16

How to Convert Prospects into Clients: The Negotiation

The process of converting a prospect into a client usually includes negotiation, which can be an uncomfortable conversation for most people in professional services. We are oriented to be helpful. We get a great deal of satisfaction from solving our clients' problems and being of service to them. We don't like playing hardball with someone who is considering a new engagement, and we don't want to risk losing goodwill. As a result, we don't ask for what we want. (Apparently, our helpful nature extends to others more than it does to ourselves.) This is why many employees earn lower salaries than they think they deserve, many professionals undervalue and undercharge for their services, and many negotiations leave money on the table.

There's nothing that says to be a helpful person, you must be a bad negotiator. If you wish to protect your fees and preserve the relationship, you must have confidence in your value and competence with negotiation techniques.

Personally, when it comes to negotiating, I have good days and bad days, though my overall confidence has improved over the years. Some years ago, I spent at least one week out of every month on the road, delivering in-person business development training programs or keynotes at partner retreats. The training programs were profitable, but the keynotes tended to be one-offs, requiring a lot of time for preparation and delivery, yielding only moderate financial upside. I consulted a few friendly competitors and discovered that my speaking fee was lower than market rates. So, on one of my confident good days, I increased my keynote fee by 50 percent, hoping it would deter lower-paying opportunities so I could spend more time at home with my wife. But it didn't have the desired effect. I received very little pushback on the fee increase. Clients continued to hire me to speak at their partner retreats at my new price. The experience boosted my confidence even more, and I started negotiating an even higher rate until I found a fair number that both compensated me properly and supported the work/life balance I was after.

NEGOTIATION TECHNIQUES

Confidence is critical when negotiating with new prospects, defending rate increases with legacy clients, or establishing expectations with sophisticated institutional clients. Without it, you may compromise, offering discounts, write-downs, and write-offs. Your clients may ask you to match your fees to lower-priced competitors, initiating a race to the bottom. But there are ways to strike a balance that satisfies their interests without compromising your own. Use these negotiation techniques to prevent your client service from becoming client servitude:

- **Know your bottom line.** Before you enter the negotiation, decide on your bottom line in terms of money and the amount of time you'll spend negotiating. After all, the longer a negotiation takes, the less time and energy you have to service your existing profitable clients or pursue prospects. With your bottom line in mind, you'll know exactly when it's time to walk away, and you'll keep the discussion from becoming unproductive.

- **Understand their expectations.** Your first objective should always be to understand the other party's expectations and budget. Without context, you may find yourself quoting a fee that gives them sticker shock. The best forum for this is a real-time conversation so that you can glean as much information about their situation as possible. *Never negotiate over text or email if you can avoid it.* During the conversation, state what you observe—if they say that their budget has shrunk, empathize with them, then ask for clarity. "It sounds like you're under some budgetary pressure. What is your allocated range for this project?" With an understanding of their budgetary expectations, you are in a better position to structure a quote they will find reasonable.

- **Ask them to advance first.** If they push back on your number and ask you to reduce it, don't respond with a lower number. First, shrink the gap by saying, "How close do you think you can come to my number?" Often, this question alone causes them to take a step forward.

- **Take incremental steps.** If their step forward isn't satisfactory, take incremental steps toward a better solution. For example, if they propose a 20 percent discount and your bottom line is 10 percent, don't start there. Offer a 5 percent discount and see if they meet you closer to your preferred number. If not, concede to 7.5 percent, 9 percent, and 10 percent. By taking incremental steps, you may retain a few percentage points you would have lost if you'd jumped directly to your bottom line.

- **Hold your ground.** If their number is still low, hold your ground. "I'm not comfortable with your proposal. Let's explore other alternatives." This opens the door to exploring mutually favorable counters.

- **Explore counters.** Explore alternatives that both protect your profit margin and enable a win for the other side. "I'm willing to give up X, as long as you throw in Y." For instance, ask if they will engage you for additional service needs at a lower rate. This counter expands the scope of your work in the future and makes the compromise more worthwhile. If they are unwilling to add tangible assets to the negotiating table, counter with intangibles that benefit you and bring the scales back into balance. For example:

  - Ask for referrals: Describe your ideal client profile to them and request that they refer you to a colleague in their network who fits that description.

  - Ask for a testimonial for the excellent work you've done for them in the past so you can use it in your marketing materials and as a recommendation on your LinkedIn profile.

  - Ask for an opportunity to present to a group they belong to, such as a trade association or roundtable.

  - Ask to be their guest at their next board meeting or social event so you can build your network with some of the people on their Short List. Obviously, you want to make ethical and comfortable requests of the client, but many of their intangibles can be of greater value to you than the discount you give in exchange.

- **Retreat as a last resort.** Generally speaking, you should only concede if you have exhausted your counters. Conceding is akin to giving the other party something in exchange for nothing. It signals that your services may not be as valuable as your pricing suggests and that a little pushback from the buyer will pressure you into compromising your pricing standards.

- **Don't settle for a promise.** Avoid acquiescing immediately to their demands in exchange for the inference that now they "owe you one" and that they'll make it up to you in the future. This vague scorekeeping introduces toxic expectations into the relationship, often leading to inaccurate assumptions, resentment, passive-aggressive communication, and future misunderstandings. They also tend to reduce the longevity of the client's engagement.

- **Be willing to walk away graciously.** If the client wants an outcome less favorable than your bottom line, be prepared to walk away graciously. Don't snub them or take on a resentful air with them. Once they shop around, they may find that your competitors are just as uninterested in an unreasonable negotiator. As they run out of viable options, they may decide to change their attitude and give another knock at your door, but only if it wasn't slammed in their face.

Negotiation Techniques in Practice

You will use only one or two of these techniques in a typical negotiation. Here are a few examples of how they might play out.

A client asks for a discount. You hold your ground and counter with value-adds that satisfy their need for a better arrangement. These include:

· A set number of pro-bono hours dedicated to the client's charity of choice.

· An educational seminar that directly addresses one of their most pressing problems.

A client asks for a reduction on the latest invoice, which is much higher due to the number of extra hours required last month. You counter with an alternative fee arrangement that includes a capped flat fee so the client can safely predict their monthly expense for the rest of the engagement.

A prospect balks at your fees. You ask about their budget—they don't have one, and because they have never engaged a firm like yours, their expectations of market rates are entirely uninformed. You hold your ground by saying, "I would like to connect you to a few companies in your industry who had similar needs before they engaged us so you can hear their perspective." After speaking with two of your satisfied clients, they adjust their cost expectations to more reasonable levels.

A client tells you they had a challenging quarter and asks you to refrain from applying your annual rate increase to their account. They suggest that if you freeze your rates with them this year, they will try to make up the difference next year. You counter by offering to defer the date when the increase takes effect by a few months. You have the fee increase you need this year, and they have less immediate financial stress.

A client says they can only continue working with you if you agree to a 10 percent discount. You explore incremental steps, but they hold their ground, so you agree to the discount in exchange for the following intangibles:

· A testimonial on the excellent work you've provided.

· A presentation to an industry trade association they belong to.

· An introduction to a decision-maker you found in their LinkedIn network.

They agree to your terms, and the decision-maker they introduce eventually becomes a great client.

As you become more comfortable integrating these negotiation techniques into your conversations, you will start to think of them as part of a game. The more you play, the more you'll find yourself winning.

Exercise: Define Your Bottom Line

 5–10 minutes

This exercise will help you establish clear boundaries, so your negotiations stay on track and your rate integrity stays intact.

Step 1: List Your Offerings

Write down a comprehensive list of the products and services you offer.

Step 2: Determine Your Bottom Line

For each offering, determine the minimum acceptable fee that you are willing to negotiate to without compromising your business.

Step 3: Determine Time Allocation

Decide how much time you are willing to spend on each negotiation before it becomes unproductive.

Step 4: Document Your Decision

Create a document outlining your bottom lines for fees and time. Keep it accessible for reference during negotiations.

Step 5: Practice

Before your next negotiation, review your bottom-line policy to reinforce your commitment to maintaining your boundaries.

Scan this QR code to download a PDF of this exercise and the corresponding worksheets.

Chapter 17

How to Expand High-Value Clients

One of the challenges I often faced as an actor was typecasting. After playing the villain in a few films and TV shows, I became known for those roles and found it challenging to secure auditions that would allow me to branch out into more diverse work. The same challenge is common in professional services. By branding your expertise, you enjoy the upside of typecasting, where your professional network consistently associates you with a particular industry, solution, and prospect, and refers accordingly. But once you've secured a client, your work with them tends to follow the same theme until you earn their confidence in your firm's other solutions.

FROM TECHNICAL EXPERT TO TRUSTED ADVISOR

A law firm once approached me to solve a client expansion problem. They had a Fortune 500 client on their roster who consistently engaged them for intellectual property work. Being a full-service firm with multiple practice areas, they were eager to cross-sell additional service lines. On a few occasions, they had requested a meeting with the client to assess additional needs and expansion opportunities, but the response was always the same: "No thanks. We'll let you know when we have another intellectual property matter." This was a classic case of typecasting, where the client thought of the firm strictly as a technical expert in one area rather than as a trusted advisor who could deliver guidance on multiple fronts.

David Maister, Charles Green, and Robert Galford coined the term "Trusted Advisor" in the book of the same name, illustrating how the key to success lies in the ability to earn greater trust and confidence from your clients over time. Only then can you graduate from engage to expand. Only then will your clients be willing to discuss higher-level issues, come to rely on your perspective, act on your strategic recommendations, and refer you with enthusiasm. The fastest way to transition from technical expert to trusted advisor begins with a constructive feedback loop.

THE THREE TYPES OF CLIENT FEEDBACK AND HOW THEY HELP EXPAND YOUR CLIENTS

As we go through life pursuing our various agendas, we occasionally lose sight of the fact that we are not at the center of the universe. Yes folks, there are other people out there whose perspectives are just as important to them as yours are to you. And the irony is that focusing on their priorities almost always brings you closer to satisfying yours.

Your clients have enthusiasms, opinions, concerns, and perspectives that are often unexplored. They endeavor to make a difference in their professional lives, navigating internal politics, sometimes sweating the small stuff, irritated when their advice is not sought out or appreciated. Sound familiar? So, if you want more of your client's attention, start by asking for their feedback on the work they currently engage from you.

Many resist the idea of client feedback. After all, what if the feedback is negative? It is particularly wounding for a product to get a poor review when that product is your expertise. But in my many years' experience working with professional services firms, negative client reviews are few and far between. Any dissatisfied clients have long since taken their work elsewhere. The ones who still work with you do so because they are satisfied with your current arrangement. And if any of them have a minor concern, it is better to nip it in the bud while the relationship is still salvageable rather than let it fester into the reason they leave.

In addition to client expansion, there are several other benefits to collecting feedback:

- **Quality of service.** Client feedback serves as a compass, pointing toward the aspects of your services that can be refined and enhanced. This iterative process ensures continuous improvement, aligning your offerings more closely with client expectations.

- **Retention.** Actively seeking and acting on feedback demonstrates a commitment to client satisfaction. By addressing their concerns and incorporating suggestions, you communicate that their experience genuinely matters to you, bolstering their loyalty to your firm.

- **Marketing.** Understanding how clients perceive your services aids in refining how you position your firm in the marketplace, conveying the value you bring. Many clients who give you positive feedback may be willing to formalize their praise into testimonials you can use in your marketing materials.

- **Innovation.** Clients can provide fresh perspectives and innovative suggestions during a feedback exercise, contributing ideas that you can integrate into new approaches and offerings.

- **Change management.** Implementing change can be slow at many professional services firms. But partners tend to pay more attention when the impetus comes from the client base with client satisfaction at stake.

- **Differentiation.** Actively seeking and leveraging client feedback demonstrates your commitment to continuous improvement and sets your firm apart from competitors who lack the courage or devotion to engage in a formal feedback process.

- **Expansion.** Often, a client feedback exercise opens an exploratory dialogue during which the client reveals challenges you weren't aware of. As a result, they may ask you to expand the scope of an existing project or help them in an entirely new area.

With so many benefits and no downsides, client feedback is essential for any firm serious about growth. There are three types of client feedback: satisfaction surveys, client service interviews, and needs assessments. While each serves a different role, they all help you gain the key ingredient required to expand high-value clients: insight into their perspective.

Satisfaction Surveys

In his book *The Ultimate Question*, Fred Reichheld introduced the idea of a survey that asks a client or customer to rank their likelihood of referring a product or service to a friend or colleague on a scale of 0–10. Promoters are those who select a high score of 9 or 10. These enthusiastic clients think highly of their experience with your firm and tend to be the most avid referrers. Passives are those who indicate a 7 or 8. They are not necessarily shopping the marketplace for an alternative but are not inclined to be particularly loyal. Detractors give a rating of 6 or lower. These clients are dissatisfied with their experience and likely complain to anyone who will listen. When firms conduct a satisfaction survey, they often include Reichheld's ultimate question to measure their client base's overall satisfaction and loyalty.

You can conduct a brief, online satisfaction survey across your client database, with the ultimate question and an additional "why" question for context. Short satisfaction surveys like these can garner a response rate as high as 15 percent among the clients who open the email, which is a sufficient sample size to assess the average client experience across the firm. Subtract the percentage of detractors from the percentage of promoters to determine your firm's Net Promoter Score® (NPS). This will give you an NPS ranging from −100 to +100.

- Poor NPS (less than 0): This means your client base contains more detractors than promoters. Firms with scores in this range struggle with high client turnover and poor brand reputation.

- Average NPS (between 1 and 40): Many firms find themselves in this zone, which means they mostly meet expectations but still have a notable number of detractors in the mix.

- Good NPS (between 41 and 70): These firms have satisfactory client service with few detractors.

- Excellent NPS (between 71 and 100): These firms have exceptionally loyal clients and enjoy high retention.

Comparing your score to your industry's NPS benchmarks can be helpful, but even more relevant is comparing your year-over-year NPS score to ensure it is trending upward. Use the same questions each time you survey your client base to ensure consistency when comparing data sets.

To identify expansion opportunities among your client base and begin the journey of improving your overall NPS score, examine each of the three respondent subsets. Your promoters are the advocates among your client base. Ask them for testimonials, references, case studies, and, if appropriate, request introductions to prospects in their network. Those with high expansion potential are most likely to consider your firm for additional services. Add them to your Short List if they aren't there already and conduct a more in-depth client service interview with them.

Your detractors are usually slow to pay your invoices, quick to criticize your work, and in jeopardy of switching to a competitor, all the while disparaging your reputation in the marketplace. Either address their complaints so their score improves or consider that you are better off without them (they're called detractors for a reason). Delegate them to a colleague or refer them to another provider who will be a better fit for them. Or phase them out through a client culling process. As you part ways with undesirable detractors, you'll enjoy your work more and have more time to expand your promoters. Many of your passives would increase their score by a point or two and become promoters if given more special attention. Select the high-value clients who award passive scores and ask them what it would take to improve their rating of your firm.

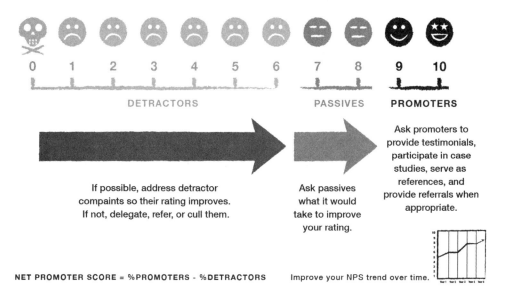

"On a scale of 0 (very unlikely) to 10 (very likely), how likely would you be to refer our firm to a friend or colleague?"

DETRACTORS PASSIVES PROMOTERS

If possible, address detractor compaints so their rating improves. If not, delegate, refer, or cull them.

Ask passives what it would take to improve your rating.

Ask promoters to provide testimonials, participate in case studies, serve as references, and provide referrals when appropriate.

NET PROMOTER SCORE = %PROMOTERS - %DETRACTORS

Improve your NPS trend over time.

Client Service Interviews

Of course, expanding work with individual high-value clients and improving your firm's NPS score requires follow-up conversations and proactive measures to enhance client satisfaction. A satisfaction survey is the first step to understanding each client's likelihood to expand, sustain, or inhibit your business. To translate this information into positive outcomes, coordinate client service interviews with your most important clients.

Kickoff the process with a strategic planning session that includes the appropriate stakeholders at your firm. Your agenda will be to facilitate candid conversations with your clients about any concerns they may be harboring, their loyalty to your firm, their pricing sensitivities, any competitive intelligence they are willing to share, and insights into how you can expand your relationship with them.

Focus on clients with solid expansion potential and a diverse mix across geographies, industries, sizes, and service needs. Include any clients who significantly influence the firm's financial performance, have the potential for additional service needs and revenue growth, are particularly susceptible to competitors, or whose scope has dwindled over time.

Craft a list of questions you can discuss with the client in thirty to forty-five minutes designed to surface the issues and opportunities most important to your firm and client service standards. Here are a few examples:

1. What concerns, if any, do you have about our services or our ability to meet your current needs?

2. How can we address these concerns to ensure your satisfaction?

3. What factors might influence your decision to continue or discontinue using our services?

4. How do you perceive our pricing in relation to the value you receive?

5. How does our pricing compare to market rates or to other vendors you use in the same service category?

6. What competitor offerings stand out to you, and how can we better compete with them?

Schedule the interviews with your client contacts over videoconference or in person so you can capture their responses and read the nonverbal cues that allude to their point of view. Compile their responses into a report to review for recurring themes and convert them into an action plan. This last component is critical, as many firms go through a client service interview process but fail to follow through on the requests received or information gleaned. The only thing worse than neglecting to solicit your client's input is asking for their feedback and ignoring it.

The feedback reports that come out of this exercise are invaluable. You will discover new opportunities to satisfy clients and expand your accounts. You may also hear recommendations on how to capitalize on previously overlooked service offerings and business opportunities.

Many of the firms we work with outsource their client service interviews to our team of consultants. As a third party, it's easier for us to probe into the details of critical feedback, ask about competitors, and ask about their likelihood to continue working with the firm. If the interviewee wants to share sensitive information, they can ask us not to attribute a specific response. That way, the firm obtains the information, and the source retains its anonymity.

Needs Assessments

A needs assessment is a unique kind of client feedback process. It's a proactive measure that helps you understand the client's business goals and the critical issues you can help them resolve. The satisfaction survey asks, "How are we doing?" and the client service interview asks, "How can we do better?" The needs assessment explores the question, "How can we better understand and serve your business given our various capabilities?" It's awkward to tack this question onto a client service interview. That's like saying, "How can we improve, and by the way, will you engage more of our services?" It's usually best to have those conversations independently. You will conduct a needs assessment primarily with your largest clients, especially the promoters, ideally soon after you've completed a successful project for them. That's when they will be most amenable to learning about the additional ways you can help them.

Any advisor who genuinely cares about their client wants to understand their business, industry, goals, and strategies. This kind of information not only helps you provide the right advice at the right time, but it also sets you apart from competitors who don't make the effort to scan the horizon and anticipate client needs.

There are a few ways to approach a needs assessment.

- **Onboarding.** You can build a few high-level needs assessment questions into your agenda with a client during the intake and onboarding process. These questions might include:

  - "What are your top three strategic priorities this year?" (If your services aren't helping them achieve at least one of them, you may find yourself in the precarious position of a one-off engagement.)

  - "What new products and services are you developing, and in what markets do you plan to sell them?" (Make sure your services are helping them succeed in this regard.)

  - "What major challenges are you facing right now?" (Some of your services may help alleviate these challenges.)

  - "Are there any significant changes on the horizon, such as a change in leadership, a relocation, or an expansion into a new geographic region?" (Any of these issues could involve risks you can help your client mitigate.)

· "In which specific areas do you see the potential for us to add more value to your business?"

Collecting this information at the outset of the engagement will elevate your perspective and advice in the near term.

- **Informal.** You can integrate needs assessment questions informally into an existing engagement simply by tying them to an external inflection point. Here are some examples:

  · A new quarter: "Given that we're entering a new quarter, I want to set up a call to understand the organization's goals for the balance of the year and ensure we're doing all we can to help you achieve them."

  · A news event: "In light of the latest industry news, I would like to schedule a call to discuss any concerns or opportunities you may see for yourself and ensure we are doing everything we can to address them."

  · An industry trend: "We have noticed an industry trend among clients in your sector that I want to bring to your attention. I would like to share some of the ways our clients are navigating the trend. What's your schedule like next week?"

- **Formal.** A formal needs assessment is the ideal forum for gathering critical information to help you expand the account. Set the client's expectations that your firm will conduct this meeting on an annual basis to ensure you continually meet their evolving needs.

By way of preparation, familiarize yourself with the latest deliverables and outcomes your firm has produced for the client. Talk to colleagues on the service team to learn if they're aware of any changes, challenges, service issues, or opportunities to recommend additional services to the client. Also, review accounting reports to see if work has increased or decreased with the client over the past two years and in which areas. If you have access to competitive intelligence, find out which other firms the client uses.

Like the client service interview, conducting the meeting by videoconference or in person is always best. If this is a large corporate client, suggest conducting the needs assessment on-site so you can also meet other people at the client company, hear their perspectives, see their facilities, and get a feel for their business, brand, and culture. You can also glean valuable information about their team. Are they over- or understaffed? Do their people look energized or disorganized? Is their work environment more traditional, or is it an informal hybrid setup? Each of these data points helps you identify new ways to help them.

- **Follow up.** Whether you gather the information during intake, through an informal needs assessment, or a formal one, send a follow-up communication within forty-eight hours, such as:
  - A thank you note.
  - Research on the client's industry or any new products or service offerings mentioned in the meeting.
  - Additional information about a specific question the client posed.
  - An introduction to someone else at the firm if the needs assessment revealed a cross-selling opportunity.
  - Next steps regarding a need you can handle for the client.

Now that you understand the three types of client feedback, you can appreciate why the law firm I mentioned at the beginning of this chapter struggled to expand work with its Fortune 500 client. The firm wanted to skip ahead to a needs assessment prematurely. If its partners had started with a satisfaction survey, they would have learned that this client is a passive, not a promoter. They could have transitioned into a client service interview to understand how to improve the client's opinion of their IP offerings and share a few examples about the other ways they have helped their clients. Only then would the client be more open to a conversation about expanding the relationship. You must earn your way to each stage of the engagement process. Your attempts to expand will fall flat whenever you push your agenda before your client, prospect, or connector is ready.

CROSS-SELLING

Once you have used client feedback or other information-gathering mechanisms to understand your client's business problems, you will be in a good position to cross-sell additional service lines that simultaneously help your clients and better leverage your firm. The recommendations in this chapter apply to a dedicated cross-selling effort between partners, or within the context of a larger client team effort.

There are many advantages to cross-selling.

- **It helps you better understand your client.** Cross-selling provides a context for exploring the bigger business problems your client may be facing, rather than those related only to your service area.

- **It increases retention.** Clients are far less likely to switch providers if they have multiple points of contact with institutional knowledge within your firm.

- **It demonstrates your commitment to client service.** A provider who seeks to help their client from every angle signals their commitment to the client's success.

- **It is easier than pitching a new prospect.** You are much more likely to secure new work from an existing client than get new work from a prospect.

- **It profits you and your firm.** Heidi Gardner's book *Smart Collaboration* illustrates just how impactful cross-selling can be. In this study, Lawyer 1 and Lawyer 2 are nearly identical (same firm, practice area, and age; and similar hours billed) except for two things: Lawyer 2 involved far more partners in and out of his practice, and the total revenue from his clients was more than four times that of Lawyer 1.[16] So, if you're looking to leverage your client base and work smarter, cross-selling is the key.

Collaboration and Business Development

Two (nearly) identical lawyers: same practice, graduation year, time with Firm, annual hours billed.

Lawyer 2's book of business is >4 times higher than his twin's.

Source: Adapted from *Smart Collaboration*, Heidi Gardner

---

16   Heidi Gardner, *Smart Collaboration* (Boston: HBR Press, 2016), 73.

Despite the many advantages and efficiencies afforded by cross-selling, a surprising number of partners hesitate to dive into the process. In our experience assisting firms in overcoming cross-selling challenges, we consistently encounter the same barrier: trust. Partners either don't trust their firms to adequately compensate them for cross-selling, they don't trust that their partners will deliver high-quality work for their client, or they don't trust that they will maintain their status as the relationship lead if they share the account with others. Sometimes, it's a combination of all three trust issues.

If you stop to think about it, all these situations are born out of the absence of a Short List. Individuals on your Short List possess the 4Cs—chemistry, character, capability, and collaboration—making them ideal cross-selling partners. If you don't feel your firm's compensation model rewards you equitably, negotiate separate arrangements with the cross-selling partner on your Short List. Given that you are both invested in a long-term relationship, you can likely negotiate an agreeable workaround. If you haven't identified firm colleagues for your Short List, consider that it may be time to make a more deliberate effort to get to know them, utilizing the techniques outlined in this book to convert at least one of them into an internal connector.

Once you've identified a cross-selling partner, you can follow these steps to begin the process.

1. **Identify the client.** Think of a promoter client with whom you've cultivated a strong relationship. A gap analysis of untapped service lines will illustrate avenues for potential expansion.

2. **Meet with the cross-selling partner.** Gather the appropriate people at your firm to discuss your intention to expand the client. If you are operating within the context of a client team,

you can collectively decide how you want the account to look in the next year to three years. If you are the sole relationship partner on the account, you can make this determination alone. Either way, the SMART goal framework will help you specify your objective. Are you looking to help the client solve a business problem through one of the service lines at your firm? Or is there a broader objective: to be selected as a preferred or panel provider so you can play a more meaningful role in their long-term growth trajectory? And what is the projected revenue to you and your firm if you achieve your intended outcomes?

3. **Create your expansion plan.** With your SMART goal in mind, document the strategies you will use to expand the account. Include a list of the people within the firm and inside the client organization who will be instrumental in achieving your intended outcomes. Will you need additional champions within the client company, looking out for your interests? (These names should eventually find their way into your Short List.) And what actions will be required? Will your expansion strategy require site visits? Educational programs? Scheduled meetings where you introduce your partners to the client? Pro bono offerings? Secondments? Who will spearhead the initiative? Is it you alone, or will others at your firm also play a role? Schedule time each quarter to review your plan and track your progress.

The most common and successful cross-selling strategy revolves around education in an area where you know the client has a challenge or need. For example, during a conversation with your client or through a formal feedback process, you discover that they plan to expand their flagship product into the healthcare industry. Based on your experience with other clients, you offer to provide a bespoke program to help them understand the relevant regulations and potential pitfalls they will need to keep in mind. You invite a partner at your firm with extensive experience in the healthcare industry to co-present with you. The client finds the program helpful, your partner adds value to the relationship, and the total revenue generated by the account increases.

The Client Expander worksheet at the end of this chapter will help you think through the cross-selling steps that maximize your leverage and minimize risks.

CLIENT GIFTING

Client gifting—whether it's to celebrate a special occasion, show appreciation for a referral received, or celebrate a successful result with a client—is a thoughtful expression of your appreciation for your client's business and, when well chosen, strengthens the connection and creates a more lasting relationship.

Most firms send the same generic gifts to everyone on their client list: the mass-produced basket of holiday goodies (even to people on a diet) or the same bottle of wine (even for those who prefer a good IPA). The accompanying card reads "Season's Greetings," often without a personalized message. It's one-size-fits-all gifting. Other firms send SWAG with their logo printed on it. That's not a gift; it's a promotional item. While mass gifting may be one of the only ways to scale such an effort across your low- and medium-value client base, you should put special effort into the gifts you send to your Short List, especially the high-value clients you want to expand.

A memorable client gift need not be extravagant; what matters most is thoughtfulness. I once sent a gift certificate to a local spa for a client who was stressed out. To this day, she thanks me for it. I sent another client a T-shirt displaying a logo from a TV show we both loved. One of my connectors often shared how stressful it was to manage his team, so I sent him a book on managing teams. I purchased a three-year subscription to *Wired* for a high-value client and fellow tech geek. The impact of these gifts went beyond any monetary value because they were personalized.

If you decide to gift, consider the recipient's cultural norms and industry regulations. In some cultures, gifting is expected. In others, it's frowned upon. Some industries impose restrictions on the monetary value of gifts or prohibit them outright. If circumstances prevent you from giving a gift, consider giving a GET—a Gesture of Extraordinary Thoughtfulness. A GET can be anything from a handwritten note expressing gratitude, a recommendation to one of your favorite restaurants, a book recommendation, or any thoughtful action you might take with a friend. GETs are the perfect follow-up action, demonstrating that you were paying attention when they mentioned that their favorite genre is mystery novels, or their favorite food is dim sum.

The key lies not in the grandeur of the gift but in the intention behind it. A well-thought-out gift or GET goes a long way toward deepening goodwill and reinforcing the relationship, putting you ahead of competitors who send a generic holiday gift basket. Again.

FACE-TO-FACE INTERACTIONS

Technology has undoubtedly improved our efficiency when it comes to staying connected. It only takes a few seconds to fire off a text or an email. It's certainly faster to set up a virtual meeting with someone than to arrange to be in the same room. But deepening your professional relationships hinges on a higher quality of interaction that only face-to-face interactions can provide.

Think about the typical virtual meeting available through Zoom or Teams. After a few perfunctory exchanges dedicated to small talk (WBT), most people launch into their agenda and "get down to business." These tightly scheduled interactions leave little room for fostering a genuine, organic conversation. By contrast, in-person meetings tend to flow in a more relaxed manner, allowing for spontaneous discussions and brainstorming. Face-to-face communication allows for richer experiences and more nuanced conversations where you can convey information more clearly and have a more memorable interaction. It also provides more details through the nonverbal cues and communication nuances otherwise flattened out by a two-dimensional screen.

The very effort itself sets you apart from competitors who can't be bothered to leave their desks and invest the time and effort in establishing a face-to-face connection with their prospects or clients. Whether it's across town or across a continent, traveling to meet a high-value client demonstrates your dedication to the relationship. It also gives you a significant advantage when pitching and closing a deal.

Plan your year so you can see your high-value clients in person at least once a year. Whether this entails attending a conference where you know your client will be, a site visit to their headquarters, or an in-person gathering for your industry roundtable, the benefits far outweigh the inconvenience.

INDUSTRY ROUNDTABLES

Earlier, I mentioned how you can use an advisory roundtable to accelerate momentum with your connectors. Similarly, professional services firms often form industry roundtables to add value to their high-value clients and attract prospective clients. This mastermind forum regularly brings together a peer network to discuss common challenges. It is an invaluable opportunity for facilitated structured peer discussions, competitive intelligence, and hyper-relevant idea sharing.

As the orchestrator of these roundtables, you set the agenda and facilitate the meetings, typically featuring a speaker or panel to attract attendance and drive group discussion. While some participants may be more forthcoming than others, those who return for subsequent meetings eventually earn each other's trust and start exchanging ideas more freely.

Successful industry roundtables are not one-off events but serialized initiatives. Consistent interaction with roundtable participants deepens relationships and uncovers opportunities for offline conversations, allowing you to explore how your firm can help further. The serialized approach turns the roundtable into a regular source for gathering valuable market intelligence and problem-solving.

For your initial meeting, begin by inviting high-value clients with whom you share strong relationships. If your Short List includes influential prospects and connectors from the industry, consider inviting them to either be participants or guest panelists. Because of your existing connection with these people, they will be more likely to sign on. Then, when you reach out to additional people you don't know as well and they ask, "Who else is involved?" you can reference a few names they might recognize. Your invitation should highlight the exclusivity of the roundtable and the compelling topics on the agenda. For example:

"I'm delighted to invite you to participate in the industry roundtable our firm will launch this year. Comprising top business leaders in our space, the group will convene quarterly for ninety minutes to delve into industry insights and discuss market-shaping issues. Our upcoming meeting features [a good speaker], leading a discussion on [a compelling topic]. Will you join us?"

After the initial meetings, a core group of active participants will naturally emerge. This core becomes the driving force around which the industry roundtable gains momentum and settles into a productive rhythm. The ongoing success of the roundtable hinges on your ability to foster engagement, curate speakers, facilitate impactful discussions, and capitalize on the expansion opportunities with the high-value clients who attend.

Worksheet: The Client Expander

 5–10 minutes

Scan this QR code to download a PDF of this exercise and the corresponding worksheets.

List your top high-value clients	Which of your services do they currently use?	Which of your other services might interest them?	Which client contact can you ask about their interest level in additional services?	Which partner would you feel most comfortable introducing to your clients?	What step can you take to move this process forward?

Chapter 18

Sustaining Momentum: A Systematic Approach to Business Development

My goal in writing this book is to share the business development distinctions they didn't teach you as you were learning your technical skills. But having the information in your head will only get you so far. The key to success is consistent action, and for that, you need to organize what you've learned into a system. So, here are the five steps for perfecting your Short List.

1. Create two or three SMART goals.

2. Compile a Short List consisting of nine to thirty-five people (clients, prospects, connectors) who can help you achieve your SMART goals. Make sure the individuals possess the 4Cs (chemistry, character, capability, collaboration) and have 3+

influence scores. 10 to 20 percent of your Short List should consist of targets who represent high-value pursuits outside your existing network.

3. Curate your Short List regularly. Use Networking Forums to find new candidates. Remove people when they no longer align with your SMART goals.

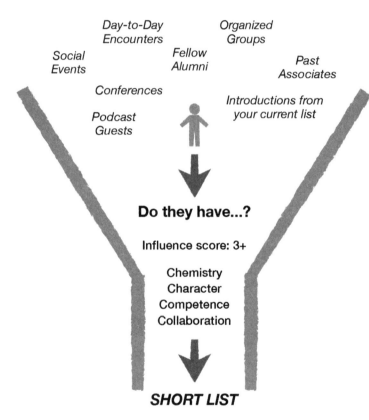

When you encounter clients, prospects, and connectors through...

Day-to-Day Encounters

Organized Groups

Social Events

Fellow Alumni

Past Associates

Conferences

Introductions from your current list

Podcast Guests

Do they have...?

Influence score: 3+

Chemistry
Character
Competence
Collaboration

SHORT LIST

4. Contact the people on your Short List monthly using the Forty Actions Matrix to advance them through the Seven Stages of Engagement.

Anticipate at least fourteen interactions before they engage.

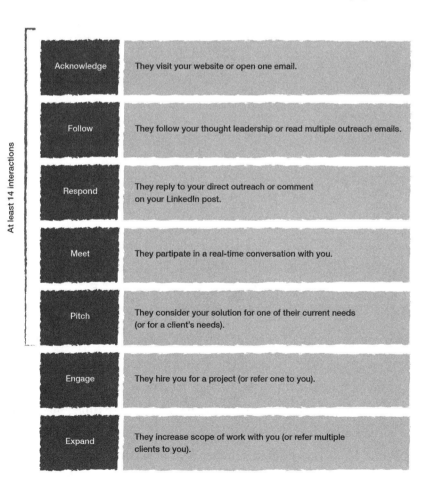

At least 14 interactions

Acknowledge	They visit your website or open one email.
Follow	They follow your thought leadership or read multiple outreach emails.
Respond	They reply to your direct outreach or comment on your LinkedIn post.
Meet	They partipate in a real-time conversation with you.
Pitch	They consider your solution for one of their current needs (or for a client's needs).
Engage	They hire you for a project (or refer one to you).
Expand	They increase scope of work with you (or refer multiple clients to you).

If your interactions are mostly virtual, arrange to see them at least once a year in person.

5. Manage your Short List with technology you will use consistently.

Sample dashboard from PipelinePlus

CLEARING THE WAY: REMOVING THE THREE BARRIERS TO BUSINESS DEVELOPMENT

Most of the people I've worked with have reasonable explanations for not prioritizing business development, even though they know it's crucial for growing or sustaining their client base. These explanations often seem to stem from external factors like time constraints or challenging market conditions. However, upon closer inspection, the real barriers are usually internal and within their control. To overcome them, we need to shift our mindsets, reprioritize, adopt more structured approaches to business development, and challenge the cultural norms that reinforce these justifications.

Barrier 1: Time

The most common objection we hear when working with our clients is, "I don't have time for business development." When you say you don't have time for something, it's a passive way of saying it is unimportant to you. If something matters to you, you prioritize it in your calendar. You make the time for it at the expense of other things that are not as important. Once people realize that business development is the key to working on more profitable projects with a higher caliber of clientele, thereby realizing their SMART goals, they make it more of a priority. But without an efficient, systematic approach, your billable quotas and a full client workload will deter even the best of intentions.

Delegation

The first time-management concept critical to business development is delegation. I've seen firsthand how difficult it is to scale without delegation. Delegating requires you to have a team you trust, clearly communicate your expectations, and show appreciation for a job well done. I've struggled with all three of these elements at some point or another.

- **Team challenges.** Many of the most satisfying periods in my career were contingent on the team I'd built at the time. I was much happier whenever I had capable people I could trust. But when I hired the wrong person for a given job, I tended to do the work myself instead of delegating, becoming a bottleneck and stressing everyone out. I learned the hard way how critical it is to hire the right team.

- **Communication challenges.** I've always considered myself a good communicator, but I have received critical feedback regarding delegation on a few occasions. I continue to work on clarifying my expectations and, especially, specifying clear deadlines for the tasks I delegate.

- **Appreciation.** One common misconception among professional services firms is the assumption that money is the primary language of appreciation among their colleagues. And yet, for all the compensation they invest in their young talent, many struggle with retention. Certainly, compensation is one way to show appreciation for good work, but in my experience, ensuring a positive work experience is just as crucial to retaining a team. Over the years, I have come to realize that our company is more profitable when we extend unlimited PTO, flexible and reasonable hours that enable work/life balance, and regular verbal praise for our teams' work.

The Art of the Gracious No

If you want more time, look no further than the word "no." Service-oriented professionals, by nature, tend to say yes to too many things. Between our natural orientation toward helpfulness and high-performance industry expectations, many of us find ourselves living overcommitted lives. Maintaining a focused Short List requires the discipline to eliminate nonessential commitments, which inevitably involves saying no. The challenge lies in declining invitations graciously, preserving relationships and reputations.

As you build your professional network, you will inevitably receive invitations to "do lunch," join a group, or participate in a nonessential activity that is only moderately of interest. Perhaps the person extending the invitation doesn't possess the 4Cs or a high enough influence score. Perhaps their invitation is misaligned with your SMART goals. Regardless, the prudent thing to do is to decline in a way that preserves your time for the things that matter to you. But conflict-avoidant professionals will either say yes to be nice or use one of these two avoidance techniques:

- **Ignore the invitation.** Ignoring someone's invitation is like saying, "Your invitation wasn't worth taking thirty seconds out of my day to acknowledge and respond." This approach may save you thirty seconds, but it lacks the common courtesy required to preserve the relationship. Your reputation is one of your most important assets in business. Ensure that people have complimentary things to say when your name comes up. You will be grateful you gave a gracious response to those who someday become gatekeepers or industry influencers.

- **Sidestep with a non-committal response.** Vague replies like, "I'll think about it and get back to you" are confusing. What are you thinking about? When will you get back to them? If you need more information, why aren't you asking for it? Of course, it's only a matter of time before they realize that what you really meant was "no" but didn't have the courage to say it. Best case scenario, they will think of you as elusive. More likely, they will regard you as unreliable.

While there is no foolproof way to reject an invitation, a gracious no is the least likely to offend. It is authentic and respectful. You begin with a compliment, acknowledging the effort put into the invitation or initiative, then, politely decline and extend your best wishes. It's simple yet powerful. Here are a few examples:

- **Networking lunch invitation:** "Thank you for your kind invitation to network over lunch. Out of respect for both of our time, I must decline as my plate is too full to accept additional networking opportunities for the foreseeable future, but I appreciate you thinking of me."

- **Advisory board offer:** "Thank you for your kind invitation to join the advisory board of your new startup. I have a great deal of respect for entrepreneurial endeavors and appreciate the amount of work it takes to get them off the ground. Unfortunately, my time constraints demand that I decline, but I wish you much success with your new business."

- **Committee invitation:** "Thank you for considering me for the firm's new committee. This will be a great initiative for the firm, and I applaud your involvement. While I believe in the cause, I cannot join the committee at this time. I appreciate being asked and wish you all the best with it."

As with any script, you should amend the wording to suit your style but follow the format of the gracious no to navigate the delicate balance between preserving relationships and avoiding overcommitment.

Inconsistency

For most people, business development involves navigating the pendulum swing between two extremes—being engrossed in client work to the point of neglecting growth initiatives, then experiencing a sudden idleness requiring an intense focus on business development. They rekindle their contacts and try to regain top-of-mind status, only to submerge into the next project, out of sight and mind. It's very difficult to maintain relationships or build momentum with this approach. Successful rainmakers run a proactive years-long marathon, not a series of reactive sprints.

Navigating the pendulum swing necessitates a balanced approach to business development. In *Atomic Habits*, James Clear emphasizes the power of incremental growth—aiming for 1 percent improvement each day. This simple principle holds profound implications when applied to business development. If you take one small action each day, representing 1 percent effort toward your objective, you make significant progress over the course of a year.

If you scan the Forty Actions Matrix, you'll see that many of them take only a minute or two to complete. During busy periods, send a quick email to touch base with a dormant high-value client or comment on a connector's LinkedIn post. When you have more time, schedule face time so you can catch up on what they've been up to while you've been underwater. On some days the full orchestra plays. On others, we hum a tune. What's important is that the music never stops.

There are many ways to integrate business development into every workday. You can insert a daily fifteen-minute calendar item dedicated to business development actions. Some prefer to schedule this first thing in the morning and get it out of the way. Others schedule it after their final meeting of the day. Either option is more effective than putting it off until there's a convenient lull.

Another efficient business development technique is to integrate it into your existing client meetings. You're already having conversations with your clients throughout the day. Before ending those calls and meetings, ask your client: "Before we wrap up, do you have an extra minute for a quick question, off the clock?" Phrasing the question this way makes it easy for even the busiest and most cost-conscious clients to grant your request. Use your additional minute to ask them a question that's easy for them to answer and allows you to help them, or vice versa. Here are a few examples:

- "I keep a carefully curated Short List of professional contacts I'd be happy to refer whenever you have a need. Are there any introductions I could make that would be valuable to you?"

- "One of my goals this year is to attend quality industry conferences. Do you recommend or attend any?"

- "I noticed a piece in the media related to your industry that I'd like to discuss with you. I think it might have interesting implications for your company. Can we schedule a separate meeting/call to speak about it?"

- "Are there any roles you're currently looking to fill? I want to keep an eye out for you."

- "How is the year progressing given the strategic priorities you shared with me a few months back? I'd be interested to know if there are any new issues or potential challenges on your mind."

Whichever path you choose, remember this: business development only occurs through communication. If you aren't making time to interact with the people on your Short List, you aren't advancing your SMART goals. Even small, incremental efforts propel you forward. Whereas you lose ground when the "too busy" narrative results in falling out of touch and allowing your relationships to atrophy.

Barrier 2: Lack of Accountability

For any potential business developer, advancing your Short List through the Seven Stages of Engagement will likely require you to do things outside your comfort zone. Chances are there is at least one person in your LinkedIn network you'd like to meet in person, but you worry that the relationship isn't strong enough, or the timing is wrong, or that you won't know how to carry it off.

It may be that you are about to do something you're not accustomed to doing, and you don't feel quite right with it. Even when you aren't aware of it, your survival instinct kicks in, and you talk yourself out of taking a risk.

> "I can't call Maggie out of the blue and invite her to lunch. She was just named CEO; she's too busy and probably won't take my call anyway."

> "That industry influencer would make a great connector for my Short List, but I'm not going to approach him. He'll think I'm being pushy."

> "There's no point in going to that conference. It will be swarming with competitors."

So, you don't do it. Why do you feel so relieved? The truth is, your uncertainty about the outcomes dissuaded you from making the call, approaching the stranger, or spending the time and money to register and attend the conference.

I should take this opportunity to confess that I struggle with this stuff, too. All. The. Time. I've gotten much better over the years, but I still occasionally talk myself out of taking the high road. Instead of picking up the phone and checking in on a client on my Short List, I'll send yet another email (even though they ignored my last two emails). The fact is, I get scared. After all, what if my call catches them at the wrong moment? What if I come across as desperate? What if they decide never to speak with me again and tell all their friends that I'm the absolute worst person in the world and I lose all my business? Then what???

Fear is part of the human experience, and it's typical to have a head full of excuses. But I've never wanted a typical life. I've always wanted an extraordinary one with exciting opportunities, an amazing team, a powerful network, and the privilege of making a meaningful difference in people's lives. I've learned firsthand that none of that comes easily. It requires an above-average effort. The average person doesn't have a productive Short List. The average person has, by definition, a middle-of-the-road network that produces mostly mediocre opportunities. When you muster the courage and focus to develop your Short List, you advance to the front of the line. You avoid the trap so many professionals fall into, allowing themselves to become perpetually busy with short-term projects so that they never have enough time to secure meaningful, long-term, career-advancing opportunities. But this superior advantage will be available to you only if you make business development more of a priority than your less ambitious colleagues. Set yourself apart by being more discerning in your choice of professional contacts and more devoted to the ones who make the grade. Today, be just a little more courageous, proactive, and patient than the norm. Tomorrow, be a little more courageous, proactive, and patient than you were yesterday. Being extraordinary requires persistent daily nudges to the edge of your comfort zone. And it makes positive change inevitable.

Of course, there will be days (sometimes weeks) when you are in short supply of courage, proactivity, and patience. During these difficult periods, it may seem like something always distracts you from picking up the phone or sending an email that reconnects you to your list. No matter how hard you try, you cannot find the time for meaningful business development. When this happens, you can use an accountability structure to get back into the game.

An accountability structure is a support system that captures your attention and prompts you to act. It can take many forms, from unobtrusive (like the display of your car's speedometer) to highly intrusive (like the flashing lights of a police cruiser in your rear-view mirror). They are both designed to raise your awareness around your driving speed, and if you ignore the first one, you will eventually encounter the other.

The key to an effective accountability structure in business development is understanding how much of an intrusion you will need to push through your reservations and maintain a consistent focus on your Short List. The section on Tracking Your Pipeline encourages software-generated email alerts for top-of-mind awareness of your key contacts. But if you find that email alerts are too easy to ignore, you may opt for a more intrusive accountability structure like a dedicated business development coach. The following section provides a range of accountability structures that can help you overcome trepidation, consternation, and procrastination.

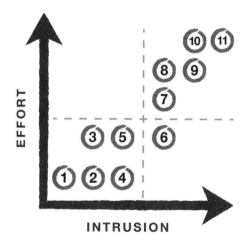

1. Set a monthly calendar reminder or recurring task to review your Short List. [Low Effort, Low Intrusion]

2. Display your SMART goals someplace where you will see them often, like a whiteboard in your office. [Low Effort, Low Intrusion]

3. Set a monthly calendar reminder or recurring task for each person on your Short List and set pop-up reminders and notifications. [Medium Effort, Medium Intrusion]

4. Use a pipeline management app like PipelinePlus Tracker to assign deadline-driven actions for each person on your Short List and enable push notifications. [Low Effort, Medium Intrusion]

5. Use a more advanced CRM solution like Salesforce to track your Short List, assign deadline-driven actions for each person, and send you alerts for each deadline. [Medium Effort, Medium Intrusion]

6. If you have an assistant, ask them to print out your Short List at the beginning of each month and place it on your desk for review. [Medium Effort, High Intrusion]

7. Establish an "accountability buddy" relationship with a connector on your Short List and schedule recurring monthly meetings to discuss your respective goals. [High Effort, High Intrusion]

8. Propose to co-author a blog series with someone on your Short List. This will require regular interaction while you are working on each post together. [High Effort, High Intrusion]

9. Organize the connectors on your Short List into an advisory roundtable that meets regularly and explores business strategies. [High Effort, High Intrusion]

10. Set a monthly coaching meeting with a colleague at your firm. [High Effort, High Intrusion]

11. Hire a dedicated business development coach to help you strategize regular outreach to your Short List. [High Effort, High Intrusion]

If the technology solutions in the lower left quadrant are sufficient to manage one of the most critical assets in your life (your Short List), then congratulations on being one of the few disciplined people who can maintain a practice with little intrusive support. But most of us are already managing so many distractions that additional reminders will only blend into the white noise that includes new emails in our inbox, emojis on our group texts, headlines from our news apps, and promotions for a new product we simply MUST try. Each notification is functionally impossible to interpret without looking, so unless we carefully curate our notifications, our attention is captured by High Intrusion, Low Effort messages all day long. To reclaim our time and focus, we must design the distractions that we want to pull our focus.

Notice that as you move higher on intrusion and effort, you move away from digital notifications and start to involve other people. Because of the personal relationships we develop with our human accountability structures, we give them more attention, are loathe to disappoint them, and are more likely to keep our word when we tell them we will take action.

Barrier 3: Firm Culture

Most professional services firms face an uphill climb when it comes to creating a healthy business development culture. Their aggregate of technical experts inherently resists the very notion of a sales culture. (Indeed, many firms consider the word "sales" to be undignified, hence my repeated reference to "business development" in this book.) Their compensation systems predominantly reward lagging indicator results (signing up a new client), never leading indicator investments (actively pursuing potential clients). Consequently, the incentives primarily resonate with those who can defer gratification, sometimes spanning several years. Even then, some firms don't adequately reward client origination or cross-selling, demotivating those who might otherwise make an effort and prompting the ambitious to seek more rewarding opportunities elsewhere.

We have observed firms evolve through five stages of business development maturity: hero, reactive, forward-leaning, committed, and collaborative.

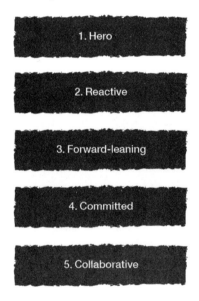

BD Maturity in Professional Services Firms

1. **Hero.** The hero firm has the least sophisticated model, with just a few rainmakers feeding the rest of the institution. This traditionalist firm focuses on maintaining the status quo

and avoids disrupting existing norms. New investments and approaches are generally frowned upon. Because the team's primary purpose is to serve the hierarchy at the top, hero firms tend to have very few rising stars with business development potential—the talent pool was not built with that skillset in mind. There is no commitment to collaboration—it distracts from short-term billing. This model leaves firms vulnerable should one of the few rainmakers leave or retire or if there is a demand fluctuation within a rainmaker's client base.

A hero firm must train the next generation in leadership and business development fundamentals to evolve to the second stage of business development maturity. When you teach burgeoning partners how to transition from a service role to a growth role, you send a clear signal that, in the coming years, they will be generating the firm's revenue, so they must evolve their leadership and business development mindsets accordingly.

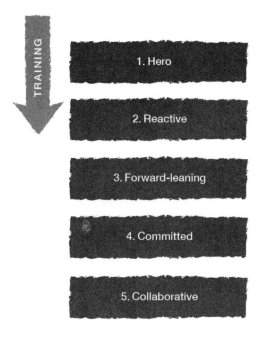

2. **Reactive.** The reactive firm may not have a cohesive plan, but it is open to minor adjustments and opportunistic about growth. If a partner from another firm is looking to make a change, the reactive firm might consider the acquisition. If a client wants to meet about expanding their relationship, the reactive firm prepares a pitch. But it will not proactively seek such opportunities with any consistent regularity, methodology, or targeted outcome.

A reactive firm will only become proactive once its partners create strategic business development plans. Only then can they orient themselves around documented strategies and targets representing a brighter future worth leaning into.

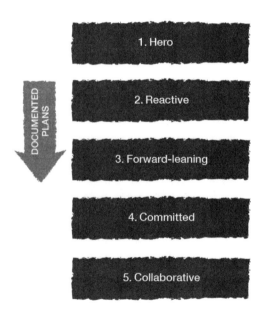

3. **Forward-leaning.** A forward-leaning firm consists of partners with documented business development plans who struggle to make the time necessary for implementation. Well-meaning partners occasionally "check in" on their plans but fail to

follow through consistently. There is some year-over-year progress in pockets, especially where coaching is in effect and growth mindsets are strong, but firmwide growth stalls due to an overall lack of meaningful commitment to change.

A forward-leaning firm demonstrates its commitment to growth when it starts holding itself accountable to business development plans. It institutes accountability structures, engages professional business development coaching, and begins to track business development activity consistently. It maintains sales pipelines. It builds and trains a team of internal BD professionals to support the execution of go-to-market objectives.

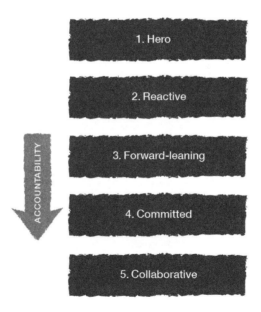

4. **Committed.** The committed firm subscribes to the adage, "You can't change what you don't measure." It has meaningful business development operational infrastructure, using technology to track pipeline activity and coaching to improve business development performance. It assigns KPIs (Key Performance

Indicators) to the various goals in its business development plans and puts initiatives in place to convert targeted opportunities. It measures progress regularly, challenging each partner to optimize their respective books of business. It also discourages the silos that prevent a team-oriented approach to growth and incentivizes cross-selling.

To fully optimize business development at your firm, you must build a culture of collaboration. Develop key client programs that expand the high-value accounts with the most significant potential for growth. Provide meaningful incentives around the leading indicators that drive a client-team approach so that everyone who works together toward a common goal is meaningfully rewarded. Firm leadership must be prepared to exit anyone who does not contribute to the firm's collaborative culture.

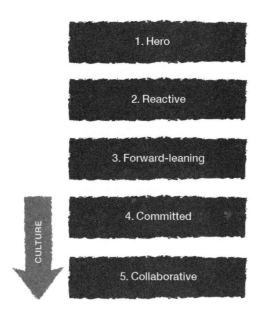

5. **Collaborative.** The collaborative firm maximizes growth opportunities at every level by acting in concert. It enforces

a strict no-tolerance policy against unproductive siloes, challenging traditional, outdated thinking models and piloting innovations from other industries for continuous process improvement. The firm leverages technology to its full potential and implements client teams across the organization, managing them effectively. Embracing business development training and coaching is a priority at all levels.

It's important to note that transitioning from one stage to the next is usually a years-long endeavor, and most firms never fully realize a collaborative culture. It is an aspirational state, difficult to achieve across all business development functions. The key is to examine each function, from staffing to compensation to technology to training, understand where you are now, and how you can advance your various components to the next stage. Perhaps you're at the hero stage when it comes to business development technology, but your cross-selling is more forward-leaning. Perhaps most of your firm's BD acumen is reactive, even though you have a few collaborative partners. In our experience, every firm has a unique blend of business development challenges and opportunities.

For most firms, initiating a formal business development training program among a cohort that currently struggles to bring in business will advance the institution's position on the maturity model. For a few virtuosos, business development is an innate talent. Rainmaking comes naturally to them and they quickly rise to positions of power and influence at their firms. In our experience, only one in ten professionals have this inherent ability. At the opposite end of the spectrum are the technicians. They would rather have their teeth drilled than even think about BD. They prefer to focus exclusively on their technical expertise, even if it means they may never have clients of their own or the professional autonomy that comes with a book of business. Approximately one in three fit this archetype. In the middle, you have your potential business developers. These professionals can build significant business books when trained and appropriately incentivized, given a process to follow and an accountability structure that sustains momentum. But left to their own devices, their outcomes will be moderate.

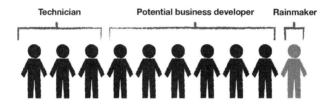

To diversify revenue at a professional services firm and to ensure it is not overly dependent on a few select rainmakers, it must provide business development training for the middle category. They will only develop rainmaker confidence if they gain business development competence.

The pages of this book illustrate how business development can be a multi-faceted, nuanced endeavor. Not only do you need to understand the various techniques involved, but through trial and error, you must customize your approach, focusing on the methods that best fit your unique personality, network, strengths, and proclivities. Reading books like *The Short List* is an excellent start, but with so much potential revenue at stake, it is prudent to invest in formal business development training programs. If you don't already have a relationship with a training provider, visit pipelineplus.com to learn about our offerings. We have trained thousands of professionals at hundreds of firms for over two decades. The most successful trainees who go on to develop significant topline growth for their firms sustain their momentum by putting accountability structures in place.

If you want to understand how this model applies to your firm's BD culture and how to advance to the next stage, use the QR code on this page to qualify for our complimentary BD assessment.

STRAIGHT TALK FOR FIRM LEADERS

Firm leaders bear the responsibility of propelling growth and advancement within their organizations. Despite this, they often find their time consumed by high-maintenance partners, their own book of clients, or firm politics, hindering their ability to drive meaningful change management. Others struggle to secure buy-in from partners who can't agree on the best way to serve the various interests at the table. Here's a no-nonsense guide for leaders to cut through the clutter and foster a culture of growth:

1. **Assess your business development culture.** Understand where your firm stands on the maturity model I outlined earlier in this chapter and identify the areas ready for evolution. Invest in your potential business developers as though the future of your firm depends on it. Occasional lunch & learns and informal mentorship programs do not meaningfully improve performance. If you want concrete results, you must institute serious training programs that accelerate revenue generation. For those high-potential colleagues poised for growth, sponsor individual coaching programs to support their transition from good to great.

2. **Understand how the following leading indicators are trending.**
   Identify where to work smarter, not harder.

   - BD pipelines: Track the number of targets each business developer has on their Short List and their ratio of low-, medium-, and high-value targets.

   - BD actions: If the overall output of your firm's business development activity is too low, use financial incentives or gamification techniques to increase the volume and quality of outreach.

   - Cross-selling efforts: Track the number of service lines sold to your top clients and ensure it is trending upward.

   - Average client value: Divide the total revenue at the firm by the number of clients to determine your average client value. Is the number consistent with the firm's target ICP (ideal client profile)? If not, start thinking about how you will close the gap.

   - Sales cycle: Measure the average length of time it takes to advance your prospects through the engagement stages. At which engagement stage does your firm experience the most significant drop-off? If the overall timeframe isn't shrinking, set expectations and challenge or incentivize accordingly.

To improve these BD metrics, hire BD-savvy professionals, give them the technology they need to track your data, and the leadership support they need to drive improvements. If your culture isn't ready to hire sophisticated BD professionals, bring in contractors who can pilot smaller growth initiatives at your firm. Be a visible growth champion, publicly acknowledging those who make the effort to advance the firm and calling out the aspects of your culture that are stuck.

Depending on the political currents at your firm, you may only be able to implement a few of these suggestions. Take whatever steps you can. As each maneuver pays off and your firm advances its position, more internal champions will emerge, eager to align themselves with proactive leaders and positive outcomes.

Exercise: Business Development Diagnostic

 **1 minute**

If you've addressed the three barriers of time, accountability, and culture to the best of your ability but find that your Short List still comes up short, run this business development diagnostic. It will help you identify which chapter from this book you should revisit for a deeper dive into its suggestions.

PROBLEM	SOLUTION	RELATED RESOURCE	CHAPTER
My SMART goals are not coming to fruition.	Review your calendar last month. How many of your meetings were with people on your Short List? 1/10? 2/10? If your goals are not advancing as quickly as you'd like, increase the ratio next month so that more of your meetings are with people who can help you succeed.	Calendar Review Exercise	4
My Short List contains too few individuals.	Attend networking forums.	Leveraging Untapped Networking Forums	9

continued

Many of the contacts on my Short List are unresponsive.	Identify those who you have not contributed to recently. Give them a personalized gift or GET.	Client Gifting	17
Business is slow.	Reach out to anyone on your Short List whom you haven't spoken to in the last month and take one of the Forty Actions with them.	Forty Actions That Advance Contacts through the Seven Stages of Engagement	12
My connectors send too few opportunities.	Form an advisory roundtable.	Advisory Roundtables	14
My connectors send the wrong opportunities.	Contact your connectors and share your latest SMART goals with them. Then, make connection requests.	Connection Requests	14
My clients generate too few engagements.	Meet high-value clients in person.	Face-to-Face Interactions	17
My largest client accounts are not expanding.	Don't assume your clients will contact you with additional issues. Assumptions are the nemesis of business development. Conduct a needs assessment of your high-value clients to better understand the issues they are currently facing.	Client Feedback	17
We need more of our people to become rainmakers.	Elevate BD mindsets at your firm through regular training and coaching programs. Put more meaningful accountability and pipeline tracking mechanisms in place.	BD Maturity in Professional Services Firms	18

Conclusion

So often, as professionally ambitious people, we feel we must put our family, friends, and even ourselves last while prioritizing our clients' needs, project deadlines, and to-do lists. But it doesn't have to be such a binary choice. The space between consists of productive, engaging conversations with a select few. Our values are aligned, we care about each other's success, and the results we produce are a celebration of the time and connection we invest in each other.

Certainly, maintaining a Short List will make you more organized and efficient. It will help you systematize your business development for more consistent effort and profitable outcomes. But ultimately, that's the trivial stuff. More importantly, it will integrate principles into your workday that make your professional life more fulfilling. When you clearly define what you want and proactively pursue it; when you communicate authentically and courageously with people you care about; when you eliminate the nonessential distractions so you can focus on the vital few who matter most; when you help others succeed and deepen your relationships with them, you set yourself up for more satisfying moments throughout the day. You just might live longer, too.

Longevity studies suggest that people who have strong social networks of meaningful relationships live longer, happier lives. In his book *Thrive: Finding Happiness the Blue Zones Way*, and separately, in his Netflix documentary, Dr. Dan Buettner provides data and case studies on communities where the average happiness and mortality rates are considerably higher than the rest of the planet. It turns out that factors like diet and pollution play a much lesser part in extending life, reducing dementia, and increasing happiness. It's the quality of their communities that plays a significant role.

This dynamic is also evident in the very shortest of Short Lists: our significant others. The Renfrew/Paisley study[17] conducted in the 1970s examined nearly 4,400 aging couples to understand the relationship between grief and mortality. They found that 68.5 percent of men and 47.2 percent of women died shortly after the loss of their spouse. Certainly, coping with the stress, grief, and trauma of losing one's life partner can drain the will to live. Still, those with more robust family and social networks were much more likely to survive bereavement than those who were more socially isolated.

It's almost as if there is a life force that is amplified through our ability to interact, help one another, and contribute. And when we become self-absorbed, lonely, and unable to interconnect, we lose some of that life force.

Which brings me back to your Short List. Life is fleeting, and

17   Carole L. Hart, David J. Hole, Debbie A. Lawlor, George Davey Smith, Tony F. Lever, "Effect of Conjugal Bereavement on Mortality of the Bereaved Spouse in Participants of the Renfrew/Paisley Study," *Journal of Epidemiology & Community Health* 6(5), 2007, https://jech.bmj.com/content/61/5/455.

time is precious. Spend what you have with the people you care about, doing the things that fulfill your personal and professional purpose. As for the rest, put it on your Long List and file it away. You can deal with it later.

Appendix

PipelinePlus Offerings

1. PipelinePlus Tracker—A simple app designed to help you manage your Short List. Firms with internal coaches also use this technology to manage pipelines, scale coaching initiatives, oversee client teams, and improve BD performance.

2. PipelinePlus Trainer—A series of video tutorials that teach many of the concepts in this book through a self-directed e-learning experience.

3. PipelinePlus Insights—Our content distribution platform delivers curated insights directly to the people at your firm, enabling them to share these insights with clients.

4. PipelinePlus Roundtables—Our executive roundtables serve as facilitated peer forums for leaders in professional services firms. These exclusive communities are ideal for idea sharing, benchmarking, and deep discussions on the critical business challenges that industry peers are uniquely positioned to understand and address.

5. Business Development Coaching—Our team of experienced BD coaches works with your team to clarify strategies, activate Short Lists, and maintain accountability.

6. Train-the-Trainer—A professional development program for internal staff interested in learning how to improve BD coaching skills.

7. Strategic Consulting—Our management consultants assist firm leaders as their organizations advance and evolve. They also regularly conduct client feedback programs that inform firm strategy.

David Ackert and his team regularly speak on a variety of topics at firm retreats and corporate events, including building influential networks, pitching, negotiation, cross-selling, and all the other concepts in *The Short List*.

Learn more about our offerings at PipelinePlus.com or scan this QR code:

Acknowledgments

For a fantastic foreword: Heidi Gardner

For editing assistance on early drafts: Olivia Watson,
Ann Norvell Gray

For guiding me through the process of finishing this book:
the good folks at Greenleaf

For cartoon contributions: William Lebeda

For generously sharing insights: Matt Toledo, Xuan Zhao,
Suzie Doran

For thought leadership: Stephen Covey, Malcolm Gladwell,
Keith Ferrazzi, Dan Pink, Adam Grant, James Clear,
Sam McKenna, Mo Bunnell, Nir Eyal

**For getting our PipelinePlus technology off the ground and
shepherding its evolution; also for helping to get the book cover
across the finish line:** Brad Brizendine

For always saying yes when I ask for help: Andrew Apfelberg,
Sally Aubury, Suzie Doran, Dave Romans, Rachel Foltz,
Justin Siegel, Michelle Iturralde

For being in my corner: Jamey Harvey, Benjamin Rosenbaum

For professional support and friendship: Jenna Schiappacasse, Justin Portaz, Darryl Cross

For decades of mentorship and friendship: Brian Napack

For helping me get my start: Bill Flannery, Larry Bodine

For being an integral part of an extraordinary team: Hannah Hasinski Smith, Kevin Martin, Mike De La Rosa, Jackie Kappus, Jennifer Castleberry, and Lauren Martinez

For providing outstanding guidance to our clients: Rich Bracken, Kathleen Flynn, Kip Guthrie, Melissa Hoff, Lindsay Hamilton, and Carmelo Millimaci

For love and support: Julian Ackert, Stephen Ackert, Shirin Tafreshi, Pouneh Rafat

For being my partner in all things: Rebecca Nassi

About the Author

DAVID ACKERT is co-founder and CEO of Ackert, Inc. and its subsidiary, PipelinePlus. He is a highly regarded business development thought leader. Over the past two decades, he has pioneered revenue acceleration programs for hundreds of professional services firms around the globe.

David regularly keynotes at partner retreats and speaks at industry conferences. He facilitates executive round-tables for managing partners and CMOs from firms across North America. He serves as a guest lecturer at USC's Marshall School of Business, Carnegie Mellon University, and at the UCLA School of Law. He holds a master's in psychology from the University of Santa Monica and is a Fellow at the College of Law Practice Management.

David volunteers as a Big Brother with the Big Brothers and Sisters program in Los Angeles.